Cambridge Elements

Elements in Environmental Humanities
edited by
Louise Westling
University of Oregon
Serenella Iovino
University of North Carolina at Chapel Hill
Timo Maran
University of Tartu

THE EARTH INTOXICATED ON IMAGINATION

Annabelle Dufourcq
Radboud University and Wageningen University and Research

Shaftesbury Road, Cambridge CB2 8EA, United Kingdom

One Liberty Plaza, 20th Floor, New York, NY 10006, USA

477 Williamstown Road, Port Melbourne, VIC 3207, Australia

314–321, 3rd Floor, Plot 3, Splendor Forum, Jasola District Centre, New Delhi – 110025, India

103 Penang Road, #05–06/07, Visioncrest Commercial, Singapore 238467

Cambridge University Press is part of Cambridge University Press & Assessment, a department of the University of Cambridge.

We share the University's mission to contribute to society through the pursuit of education, learning and research at the highest international levels of excellence.

www.cambridge.org
Information on this title: www.cambridge.org/9781009644426

DOI: 10.1017/9781009420006

© Annabelle Dufourcq 2025

This publication is in copyright. Subject to statutory exception and to the provisions of relevant collective licensing agreements, no reproduction of any part may take place without the written permission of Cambridge University Press & Assessment.

When citing this work, please include a reference to the DOI 10.1017/9781009420006

First published 2025

A catalogue record for this publication is available from the British Library

ISBN 978-1-009-64442-6 Hardback
ISBN 978-1-009-41999-4 Paperback
ISSN 2632-3125 (online)
ISSN 2632-3117 (print)

Cambridge University Press & Assessment has no responsibility for the persistence or accuracy of URLs for external or third-party internet websites referred to in this publication and does not guarantee that any content on such websites is, or will remain, accurate or appropriate.

For EU product safety concerns, contact us at Calle de José Abascal, 56, 1°, 28003 Madrid, Spain, or email eugpsr@cambridge.org

The Earth Intoxicated on Imagination

Elements in Environmental Humanities

DOI: 10.1017/9781009420006
First published online: July 2025

Annabelle Dufourcq
Radboud University and Wageningen University and Research
Author for correspondence: Annabelle Dufourcq, adufourcq@hotmail.com

Abstract: The aim of this Element is to forge new conceptual tools to give more ecological power to the human imagination. Imagination, both an innovative force and one that distances and blinds, is central to the ecological crisis as well as its potential resolution. Human imagination creates a bubble of denial, fostering the illusion of a smooth, reassuring, controlled, and neatly compartmentalized world. This Element critically contrasts the harmful modern concepts of reality and imagination with a more grounded "earthly" and "animal" imagination. It proposes to overcome the tension between two currents in environmental thought: those advocating imagination for utopian transformation, and proponents of realism, urging confrontation with the material world beyond anthropocentrism. Through analysis of key contemporary environmental work alongside insights from ethology and biosemiotics, the Element underpins the concept of "animal imagination," offering an alternative approach to environmental imagination and activism that fosters deeper engagement with the living world.

Keywords: imagination, realism, earth, animal, ecology

© Annabelle Dufourcq 2025

ISBNs: 9781009644426 (HB), 9781009419994 (PB), 9781009420006 (OC)
ISSNs: 2632-3125 (online), 2632-3117 (print)

Contents

1 Introduction 1

2 Calling for More Imagination 13

3 Calling for More Realism 19

4 A Destructive Debate 28

5 What Went Wrong with Human Imagination: Lessons from Shakespeare's *Tempest* 35

6 Ecological Imagination: Animal Imagination 47

7 Animal Imagination and Activism: Magic Now 58

8 Conclusion 67

References 70

1 Introduction

The aim of this Element is to forge new conceptual tools to give more ecological power to the human imagination. Our goal is to figure out how humans can invent an alternative to an environmental degradation that today appears as a massive and inescapable *reality*, without falling into denial and anthropocentrism.

This Element originates from the realization of an insufficiently addressed tension within the environmental humanities. Two tendencies are emerging concurrently: environmental imaginarism and realism. Though not formalized schools of thought, they embody two conflicting poles of the climate crisis.

The first tendency, exemplified by Ursula K. Le Guin and Amitav Ghosh, considers imagination as the key to a proportionate response to the ecological crisis: We urgently need to reimagine our world from the ground up as only a new worldview can radically overturn the system we are now stuck in. According to these "imaginarists," imagination – defined as the ability to think freely beyond the rigid constraints of our current reality and to envision alternative possibilities – is crucial in overcoming the crisis. Their argument closely aligns with the principles of deep ecology defined by Arne Næss (1973), emphasizing that we must dismantle the pervasive anthropocentric and consumerist worldview that normalizes the exploitation of nature. From a deep ecological perspective, imagination becomes central as the faculty that shapes reality itself: We must first transform our minds, since our thinking constructs the reality we inhabit. In this sense, deep ecology represents an idealist rather than a realist approach.

The environmental realist tendency, in turn, is characterized by the reference to a reality beyond human comprehension and independent of worldviews. As I will show, it draws on the motley philosophical and literary legacy of realism in various ways. It manifests through the following key traits: A rejection of the realm of representation and imagery, a focus on direct action, and a portrayal of thinkers as bodies that act rather than as imagination that makes sense of the world.

In the *Manifesto of New Realism* (2020), Maurizio Ferraris explains that the urgent need for realism emerged in the early 2000s as a response to postmodernism that dominated the twentieth century and posited that all is interpretation and that there is no escape from this symbolic realm of representations. The need for realism is particularly acute in the post-truth era and the climate crisis. As Kate Soper notes, "It is not language that has a hole in its ozone layer" (1995: 151). Controversies over various systems of interpretation undermine the credibility of objective scientific knowledge just as scientists are sounding the alarm and the climate emergency exposes reality's resistance to being shaped or reinterpreted at will. It is therefore not surprising that Dipesh Chakrabarty, who coined the concept of the planetary age – an era marked by humanity's realization that Earth exists beyond human experience and agency – refers to Quentin Meillassoux, the leading figure of the return of realism in the 2000s, when he defines the planet as "anterior to the emergence of thought and even of life – *posited, that is, as anterior to every form of human relation to the world"* (Chakrabarty 2021:87; Meillassoux 2009:10).

From this environmental realist perspective, the human imagination is regarded as central to the crisis itself. The imagination, as the capacity to detach from the given and focus on the absent or unreal, has the power to estrange humanity from reality. It must indeed be held responsible for both the pharaonic projects and the denial, the truly delusional blindness that now endanger the planet. The meme "This is fine" and the film *Don't Look up*, both viral figures in contemporary culture, highlight that humans today are struggling with the loss of contact with reality and accuse the ruling elites of being stuck in a phantasmatic bubble of glamorous images and reassuring words. Bruno Latour tackled this problem by claiming that different parts of the population now live on irrevocably different planets, making it impossible for figures like Thunberg and Trump to understand or reach each other (Latour 2020b). Yet, Latour argues that these "planets" are not equally virtual. Despite initial European denial in March 2020, COVID did not remain a Chinese problem. Climate skeptics notwithstanding, Earth's surface temperature has risen by 0.08°C per decade since 1880. Many scholars have thus placed the concepts of reality and realism at the core of their environmental discourse. I will particularly examine the contributions of Carol Adams, John M. Coetzee, Cora Diamond, and Bruno Latour in Section 3.

While both approaches present promising solutions to the environmental crisis, they also expose significant limitations within their respective projects; hence, this Element claims that a key environmental issue today is the intoxication of the Earth on imagination, which takes two key forms.

First, the Anthropocene is inextricably linked to hegemonic fantasies that have become all-pervading, blinding, and addictive, while threatening the integrity of the planet. The dream of human superiority and control over an ordered nature lies at the heart of the Anthropocene; it relies on myths and propaganda that assert the objectification and mechanization of nature, the glorification of the rulers, and the vilification of the exploited. Abundant literature in environmental humanities connects the climate crisis and the systematic development of racist, speciesist, sexist constructions as essential for liberating the forces of exploitation and overproduction.[1] The Anthropocene dream reshapes real space to mirror its vision with eerie precision: Societies and landscapes are compartmentalized, land is seized for controlled production, and concrete spreads to enforce order. Every corner of the planet is absorbed into enthusiastic overproduction and acceleration that seem unstoppable, while the earth and people burn out. As this anthropocentric dream has become the perfect cover for a multi-traumatizing structure, people have grown increasingly numb to pain and injustice. Doubts and dissatisfactions are easily channeled through industrially produced films, media, and social media, which process these feelings in endless cycles of superficial, polarized images, and debates. The Anthropocene is the Earth really shaped by a powerful human imagination turned hegemonic.

Second, even the possibility of an alternative to the Anthropocene dream grows from the heart of the imaginary realm. Both the call to imagine new worlds and the call to realism belong in the realm of tentative and elusive representations. They develop through mediums that bear all the marks of human passion for symbols and images, thus aggravating our disconnection from the Earth. Millions have watched *Don't look up*, a biting denunciation of climate denial: Does that make us climate change heroes? Watching a movie does not equate to action; streaming perpetuates excessive energy demand, and Netflix is still a profit-driven business. Even the call for realism – returning to the body and the planet – still carries the weight of imagination. Too many words, too many representations, too much complacency toward fancy images: Damage control, marketing operations, communication campaigns, endless debates, viral infections of lies, myths, and pernicious theories undermine contemporary attempts to address the crisis in a way proportional to its *literal* seriousness.

Similarly, activism today is torn between the weakness of sheer violent action – a brute reality that can in fact easily be reframed and repressed by state authorities as eco-terrorism – and the need to develop new utopias and symbolic actions designed to revitalize people's imagination and therefore vulnerable to being recuperated and recoded by hostile ideologies. Marketing campaigns around the climate emergency are abundant, with greenwashing becoming increasingly prevalent. While eco-activism opposes these deceptive practices, it often must rely on advertising tools that are homogeneous with them. To what extent do these representations and awareness-raising efforts serve as genuine catalysts for change, or are they merely simulations of action?

---

[1] This literature is too extensive to cover here. For representative works, see Blaut (1993), Plumwood (1993), Yusoff (2019).

This Element will show that even realism operates as a rhetoric rather than a simple return to reality. Such a return is, in fact, challenged by the very behavior of the Earth. Both contemporary stochastic approaches and the Gaia model of the biosphere indeed demonstrate the impossibility of ascribing stable, objective properties to the planet. I will refer to this as the "odd Earth" – a "reality" with the fluid, shifting nature of fancies.

By examining the tensions between environmental realism and imaginarism, along with the resulting aporias in contemporary environmental studies and activism, this Element demonstrates why current concepts of reality and imagination hinder effective approaches to the climate crisis and need substantial reworking. I will argue that a fundamental dimension of imagination vital for addressing the crisis is systematically overlooked and repressed by the Anthropocene: The animal imagination, distinguished by its perspectival plurality, embeddedness, and empathy. The aim is to show, first, that imagination is not an exclusively human faculty, but arises from the imaginative powers of the environment itself and of nonhuman beings. Second, animal imagination should not be mystified as a supernatural ability, a kind of sixth sense unique to Nature and natural beings. It is, still, we will argue, a form of magic – as it involves risks, creative leaps into the unreal, and resistance to rationalization. Yet it unfolds through gradual adjustments, vulnerable attempts, and exploratory relationships with other subjects whose interests and perspectives are to be recognized as never fully or clearly given to us. Hence, animal imagination is always embedded in concrete mutualistic relationships and inseparable from empathy, while the latter becomes abstract and blind without it.

I mentioned earlier that contemporary environmental activism is grappling with difficulties reflecting the tension between realism and imaginarism. To better understand the pitfalls to avoid, and the concrete problems this Element aims to address, we will first examine how these difficulties manifest. The introduction will then offer preliminary reflections on the concepts of reality and imagination. Finally, I will outline the structure of the sections in this Element.

1.1 Environmental Studies, Activism, and the Problem of Forceful Actions

The reference to activism is inseparable from environmental studies. In the context of the current climate crisis, there is a fundamental tendency to move away from empty words and analyses of texts and theories, because the urgency of the climate crisis compels us to be effective here and now. In short: *Less talk more action* (Mitra 2019). Commenting on the emergence of ecocriticism,

Jay Parini (1995) thus points out that "Environmental studies marks a return to activism and social responsibility (...) Students like it because it taps into some very basic concerns, and teachers of literature like it because they're bored with theory. Literary theory wasn't real. Nature is tangible."

Conjointly, on the side of environmental activism an even stronger call for reality-changing action arose. During the past recent years, prominent environmental movements such as Extinction Rebellion have largely prioritized direct action. Based on the observation that indirect efforts – such as negotiations, legal channels, or lobbying – have often failed due to the unreliability of the established system and the diversionary tactics of those in power, the direct action movement advocates for disruptive interventions against the target of protest. These actions typically involve immediate, often physical, measures designed to create an impact that cannot be easily ignored or minimized. However, recently the "We Quit" statement published on the XR website sounded like a thunderclap: The movement announced that it was abandoning direct action for the time being, because the need for change is more radical than ever, and in spite of past actions "very little has changed" (Extinction Rebellion 2022). XR is not abandoning the struggle, but is looking for action that will involve a greater number of individuals, the community in all its diversity as a whole, and must therefore temporarily renounce antagonizing disruptive action. The issue here is the elusive nature of reality: How can we act on it? How can we reconcile the need to highlight the urgency and concrete nature of ecological damage with the need to change minds and worldviews in order to change the world?

In this context, the passion – very human – for imagination is both an asset and a liability for ecological activism.

Radical ecology engages with imagination in two main ways. First, it calls for a complete paradigm shift, arguing that reality crystallizes from and owes its very substance to what I referred to as the Anthropocene dream. The perception of what surrounds us and the way our bodies have learned to live and feel, even to function, are imbued with a noxious ideology. Radical ecology claims to substitute a still-unreal-world to the rotten-to-the-core extant reality and therefore appeals to the imagination. In opposition to the realist mantra "there is no alternative," which epitomizes an alleged obdurate reality, many environmental activists seek to create a new reality that will not compromise with the existing one in any way. Further, by emphasizing the plasticity of reality and its connection to human interpretations, radical ecology also challenges the notion of an objective reality to which we should simply resign ourselves. Although we will have to qualify this first description of the imaginary dimension of radical ecology – since the new reality somehow emerges from the current one – this revolutionary stance explains why utopian and science fiction discourses are prominent in radical ecology.

The second link between imagination and ecology lies in the central reference to Gaia. Radical ecology points to a deeper reality that has been negated and repressed, but never fully destroyed. "We are the rebellion *of the Earth* [*Les Soulèvements de la Terre*], so our movement is simply indestructible," French activists claimed after being accused of violent acts against people or property and threatened with the dissolution of their organization (Del Fa 2023). The reference to the (capitalized) Earth implies a holistic and somehow animistic perspective: The Earth is deemed here as a whole that possesses its *own* interests, tendencies, and agency. The Earth fights back (Latour 2018:20) through floods, global warming, or tornados; it resists the anthropocentric plan to reduce it to commodities and exploitable resources.

In this framework, the Earth, also called Gaia, occupies an ambiguous position between the real and the imaginary. Although the mythical figure of Gaia places nature in the vicinity of witchcraft and magical practices – I will come to that in Sections 5 to 7 – it is presented by many thinkers in both environmental humanities and contemporary sciences as the key to the real world.

In Greek mythology, Gaia is the primordial principle that fertilizes itself, personifying the Earth as the ultimate mother who gives birth to all beings. She made a surreal return to contemporary Western culture through James Lovelock's *Gaia hypothesis* (1979), which posits that Earth functions as a self-regulating whole: All organisms and environments co-evolve within, contribute to, and ultimately benefit from a global system that seeks to establish and maintain optimal conditions for life.

The Gaia hypothesis did not meet with unanimous approval. While Lovelock (1988:235) clarified that he used Gaia as a metaphor for Earth's emergent stability, critics question whether this "wholeness" is a scientific or merely speculative construct. Today's research, however, must reckon with a growing number of scientists who integrate the Gaia hypothesis into their theory. To be sure, modern science is based on the principle that things, milieus, and living beings can be theoretically and physically broken down into rearrangeable building blocks, to suit the human needs. This model of a soulless and inert material world, knowable and thoroughly manageable via calculation and fragmentation, makes Gaia a childish myth or a lax metaphor. But modern science itself has eventually rediscovered that wholes are greater than the mere sum of their parts. This can be seen, for example, in the autopoietic dimension of living bodies, expressed in the plasticity and relative unpredictability of anatomy, metabolism, and behavior, also known as the vicariousness of functions and polyvalence of organs. Thus, for instance, when one area of the brain is damaged, another part creatively takes over the function that was achieved by the former (Frisch 2014). The study of global self-sustaining balance in living beings and ecological milieus provides serious arguments in support of the Gaia hypothesis.

Yet an internal tension endures as Lovelock retains the ambiguous "Gaia" metaphor over the years, referring to Gaia as an organism – albeit, amazingly, one of a different nature than all known organisms (Lovelock 1988:41). Many scientists criticized this as a reintroduction of an intangible teleological perspective, which modern science excludes on principle. Lovelock (1988:33–9) attempted to rebut accusations of teleology by emphasizing Gaia as a mathematical model of feedback-driven homeostatic tendencies. Nonetheless, he co-authored several articles with Margulis, who advocated for an autopoietic and even cognitive definition of the activity of biotas (Onori & Visconti 2012:380–2). Moreover, the mathematical model of feedback loops, when applied on a planetary scale, fails to provide a falsifiable theory (Kirchner 1990).

Beyond Lovelock, the figure of Gaia has become central in the environmental studies: It has been the subject of numerous debates about its exact nature – scientific or/and mythical, metaphorical and/or literal (Abram 1991; Latour 2019; Volk 2006) – and has also become a prominent symbol for a contemporary ecological activism that wants to underline how much the Anthropocene upsets the general natural *balance*. As the human hypergrowth project encounters environmental resistance, it reveals a contrasting picture of Gaia's *own orientations*, which conflict with the general direction of the Anthropocene.

But what does Gaia actually prefer? Is her alleged intrinsic equilibrium a tangible reality, or merely the constructs of an advanced human mind steeped in symbolic thinking? The activists' claim that they embody the Earth's rebellion, and therefore that their movement is indestructible, presupposes what it seeks to establish. The deduction is flawed: the Earth – whether as an ecosystem capable of supporting life or as a planet – is, and this is precisely the problem, destructible.

In this context, *The Rebellion of the Earth* suffered a major setback in 2023. A large-scale protest march was organized by the movement against the construction of water reservoirs of enormous capacity designed to collect water from underground aquifers for the exclusive use of a few industrial farmers. Initially, some protesters in Sainte-Soline planned to "break through the lines" (Les soulèvements 2023) meaning they intended to use their numerical advantage to apply pressure on security cordons and breach the police lines to enter the restricted area. However, not all participants were enthusiastic about the idea of using such a method. "Breaking through the lines" is both a symbol and an exercise of brute force. It signifies entering battle, and it establishes itself in the realm of raw reality. However, the government used this to its advantage: As "hostile hordes" were preparing, 6,000 policemen were fielded in the operation, armed with weapons of war, and backed up with a well-trained speech of legitimacy. Many protesters were seriously injured, and the wooly debates about alleged "eco-terrorism," skillfully fueled by the authorities, confused the message the activists were trying to convey.

So, should future demonstrations be limited to symbolic methods that were also part of the Sainte-Soline march, such as waving signs and flags, carrying large wooden sculptures of animals and chanting slogans? Is it possible to refer to Gaia without resorting to myths, images and, even more concerning, irretrievably weak fantasies? Now the question remains: Where will the power of this ecological movement come from? How can it change the real course of events? In the Anthropocene, the Earth has lost many battles against the Promethean projects of Western societies. What can be the strength of an ecosystem that is precisely a fragile equilibrium, in which each element potentially offers a new vulnerability that could weaken the whole? The challenge we face today is to empower a planet and its rebellion, both of which are inherently weak and can only be ecologically sustainable if they remain so – specifically, if they avoid resorting to the weapons of their adversaries – and yet prevail. This is the conundrum that this Element seeks to solve.

1.2 Preliminary Considerations for Ecological Imagination: The Modern Concepts of Reality and Imagination

We are concerned here with the tensions in contemporary environmental humanities between the pursuit of greater realism and the stubborn return of the curse of imagination. We must challenge the conceptual framework that prevails in Western societies and makes the problems outlined earlier intractable. Let us explain some basic definitions so that the reader can get a sense of the conceptual background on which modern Western cultures stand and from which we must start.

(1) "Reality" generally designates the state of things as they actually are, which resists our whim, exists, and unfolds independently of any subject's perception and desire. (2) By extension, the realist position and the Western concept of reality have evolved over the centuries to the model of comprehensible and controllable causal chains, implying that the state of things as they actually are is identifiable, circumscribed, graspable, and effective. Reality in

German, *Wirklichkeit*, thus comes from wirken: Work, act, produce effect, and in medieval Latin *reālitās* denotes a legally established property.

Historically, realism has been accompanied by a competition to define *true* reality or, so to say, irony intended, *the real real*. For example, modern science contrasts the color I perceive and the color as the vibrational frequency of the light wave. The latter is objective and measurable, the former is elusive and a psychological phenomenon rather than a property of the thing itself. But the second definition of the real nature of color is no less a human construction than the first, as it cannot be separated from a scientific theory or from measuring instruments developed in a particular cultural epoch. All who call for more realism should be aware of this danger: The term "reality" commonly triggers arguments that start from a demand for purification – a demand to reach the real real – that nails us down to a vain quest. The latter is typically modern: Obsessed with being at the vanguard of progress toward the truth, it often must offset its own limitations with rhetorical tricks. Is this really the basis on which we want to start the fight to get out of the bubble of denial?

Just as this Element intends to question and reframe the existing concept of reality, it concerns itself with the limits of the existing concept of imagination as it is used in contemporary debates about the environmental crisis.

The existing concept of imagination is one of the cornerstones of modern Western culture. It contains three interrelated problematic statements about the relationship between humans and the world: Imagination is a mental faculty (psychologizing the concept of imagination), it is essentially human (anthropocentric view of imagination), and it disconnects humans from nature (a stance I call the "gnostic hypothesis").

Imagination is the ability to detach from the given reality and experience or represent fictional phenomena (if you are reading a fantasy novel) or phenomena that are not present to our perception (for example, if I imagine what my friends are doing right now in their house in the woods on the other side of the world). Unlike theoretical or conceptual thinking, imagination involves a quasi-experience where the imagined object feels as if it were physically present, in flesh and blood. In other words, the imagined object appears embodied both spatially and temporally, through the experience of its sensory properties. This embodiment gives imagination its power: Some fantasies and dreams can be extremely vivid and even life-changing. Nevertheless, imagination differs from perception, that is, the sensory experience of something actually present; in this sense, imagination involves re-presentation, distance, and the splitting of the subject: I am seated on this couch, reading a book, *and* I simultaneously live adventures – *as if* they were real – in the world of chimeras and dragons.

A widespread tendency in modern thought understands imagination and its object and correlate, the imaginary realm, through a psychologizing and inwardizing approach (Sepper 2015:27–30). Images and fantasies are defined as thoughts and mere projections that manifest our emotional and mental world. Accordingly, adults accept to go through "reality testing," while immature people persist in believing that what they imagine is real, thus failing to recognize the difference between the *external* and *internal* worlds, to use Freud's terms, which have largely permeated popular psychology today.

A brief history of the modern concept of imagination shows that, alongside its psychologization and inwardization, a prevailing thesis defines overabundant imagination as the hallmark of human freedom.[2] This assertion was already conveyed by the myth of Prometheus: While Epimetheus gave creatures natural tools, humanity alone lacked real talents, a gap filled by Prometheus, who gave us the ability to invent limitless techniques. Against all odds, the lack of a particular talent is then turned into an advantage. Humans throw bridges over the void and constantly learn by trial and error, without guarantee. This ability to invent endlessly is real, but its power lies in not being bound in advance by fixed reality: It is open to anything. Human inventions are magnificent structures of emptiness, with financial bubbles as an extreme example: Born from audacity and fanciful ideas, they shape unexpected forces in the material world but remain in precarious equilibrium. Catastrophic collapse thus haunts Promethean societies.

Finally, defining imagination as an exclusively human mental faculty leads to the experience of disconnection from nature and threatens the entire scientific enterprise. Indeed, the link between knowledge and imagination is also a *topos* in Western culture: Knowledge unfolds because I can step outside the world's flesh and the stream of sensations that engulf my consciousness and thus put the world in front of me. In this way, I select a few aspects of focus, push many others in the background, refer to what this object was and will be, thereby making it a recognizable circumscribed entity. This definition of knowledge inevitably leads to Kant, that is, to the assertion that what we call real is itself the correlate of our human thought structures, and that we will never step out of this bubble of anthropocentric representation. Imagination as *Einbildungskraft* (the word Kant chose to designate imagination as a faculty that is instrumental in the

---

[2] Aristotle initiated the psychologization of imagination but saw it as a trait of life, not the human. He defined intellect as properly human – a view echoed in early modernity, where thinking in images appears ambiguous: essential in mathematics and science yet (too) corporeal and limited. From Kant, through German Idealism and Romanticism, to existentialism, it becomes a recurring theme to claim that creative imagination is central to human intelligence, radically freeing it from the given.

creation of knowledge: The spectacular power [*Kraft*] to tear oneself away from the given) is also key to the narrative of the human's separation from the Earth. I will call this narrative *the Gnostic hypothesis*, in reference to the philosophical-religious school of antiquity that contended that this world was created by an evil god and humans were thrown on earth where they could only suffer. In the Gnostic theory, a limited number of humans are connected to the "other" God, the good God; for they carry in them the spark of spirit that opens them to justice and knowledge, they will always feel alien to what surrounds them. Now, what is the connection between this Gnostic hypothesis and the psychologization of the concept of imagination? The human is, as it were, in exile in the universe of ideas, where she blossoms, in a movement of radical estrangement from the surrounding reality. Imagination, as a capacity of nothingness (Sartre 2004:186–7), is also the key to a narrative through which some humans secede and fall prey to a complex of both inferiority and superiority: Everything is possible ... but everything that humans produce is in reality *nothing*. Imagination is classically the greatest pride of modern Western humanity and its direst curse. We must therefore be careful when we sing the virtues of utopia and imagination in activism: This reference is undermined and can backfire.

1.3 Structure of This Element

The second and third sections of this Element examine the arguments exchanged in the debate between proponents of realism and advocates of a utopian approach to environmental undertakings. I will focus particularly on Amitav Ghosh, Ursula K. Le Guin, Margot Norris, Cora Diamond, Bruno Latour, and John Maxwell Coetzee.

With the latter's work, it appears that this tension between imaginarism and realism is the symptom of a deadlock rather than progress toward a solution. Indeed, as explained in Section 4, Coetzee's *Elizabeth Costello* proclaims a will to realism, while it becomes increasingly clear that a wild imagination is taking over in the innermost recesses of Costello's ideas. In the same vein, we examine in Section 4 how Latour's work gets mired in a shaky attempt to hold realism and constructivism together.

The imaginarism/realism opposition is a fruitful, but limited, tool. I am not interested in creating strawmen: All of the authors mentioned in this Element make crucial contributions to circumscribing what is deeply at stake in the climate crisis, but I contend they are all hindered by insufficiently questioned concepts of imagination and reality. In the fifth section, the roots of the sterile tension between realism and imaginarism are investigated. I argue that our civilization deals with imagination in an ecologically deeply problematic way: There are two imaginations that are commonly conflated, so that the issue of ecologically good and bad uses of imagination has so far remained unaddressed. I refer to these two imaginations as Sycorax and Prospero, for these characters of Shakespeare's *Tempest* bear the marks of an ancient and still living representation of imagination in the Western culture. *The Tempest* was written just when the Anthropocene dream was forming and it is both central to the philosophy of imagination and to recent post-colonial environmental literature. It thus gives us a unique insight into the behind-the-scenes formation of the concepts of reality and imagination and their crucial role in the climate crisis.

Prospero is presented as the imagination of manipulation and simulacra; he seeks subjugation. He is classically regarded as the epitome of imaginative powers, but he only embodies a certain, particularly effective, and dangerous, form of imagination. Prospero creates illusions and pulls the strings behind the scenes. But he prevails because he enslaves, steals, and slanders. Sycorax and her son Caliban, on the other hand, are often regarded as roughly symbolizing indigenous and matrilineal intelligence of the environment. Building on the work of Silvia Federici, Section 5 shows that Sycorax's knowledge takes the form of magic powers and imagination as the ability to awaken imaginative forces in nature. Sycorax's legacy to Caliban is indeed an "earthy" magic based on the knowledge of the island, and Prospero needs Sycorax's magic to gain power. Without this earthy imagination, the "heavenly" human imagination would be nothing. What we learn from the Sycorax/Prospero distinction is that nature is magical, that the war between Sycorax and Prospero results from the anthropocentric gaze, and that it is possible and necessary to imagine in a way that reconnects us to the Earth but is intrinsically weak, which the next sections further explain.

Sections 6 and 7 focus on the study of Sycorax, the forgotten imagination. Section 6 explores the roots of human imagination in animal imagination. It argues that nonhuman animals already develop complex imaginations, through which they organically shape their environment and interact with it, and that imagination is grounded in a non-deterministic Earth – the "Odd Earth" – particularly in animal engagement with the semiosphere and the multiplicity of interpretations and meanings that constitute a *pluriperspectival* Earth. Animal imagination, characterized by embeddedness and empathy, shows that there is a way to understand imagination not as something that separates us from nature, but rather as the tool for engaging nature accurately and with a non-imperialist effectiveness. To some extent, this approach returns to Latour's model of democratic dialogue except that we do not anchor it in a typically human political representation but in an art of negotiation, risk-taking, empathy, and mutual aid in adversity that is characteristic of the imagination of living beings in their interactions with each other and their milieu.

Section 7 revisits the challenges facing environmental activism and analyzes new practices, fueled by animal imagination, that outline a promising response to the difficulties presented in this introduction.

2 Calling for More Imagination

Imagination, as the ability to think creatively and embodiedly, is especially required to adapt to new situations and meet the challenges of unprecedentedly risky circumstances. In order to live up to a world where all ecological balances have been disrupted and the escalating impacts of climate change make prediction more difficult than ever, imagination becomes a crucial skill. Hence Schneider-Mayerson and Bellamy propose an *Ecotopian Lexicon* (2019) to counter our current "inability to imagine another path forward." Their stated goal is to resuscitate our imaginative abilities by unlocking and expanding the language we use to describe "the present-day crisis and its possibilities." Only imagination seems to have the power and the tear-away capability to create the way to a new world and "rethink what we resign to inevitability" (Hsu 2020). This call to imagination also applies to the contemporary sciences, as Thomashow argues in *Bringing the Biosphere Home* (2002). The sciences need the imagination that is at work in art to develop new paradigms: Scientists and laypeople should dare taking "leaps of imagination" to think on the scale of the universe and bridge "local and global, the past and future, the organism and the environment," thereby moving "through ecological and evolutionary space and time" (Thomashow 2003).

In this section we will focus more specifically on the strong trend toward fantasy that operates in contemporary environmental studies and especially in environmental humanities and ecocriticism, as they emphasize the role of competing worldviews and narratives in the climate crisis. Ghosh and Le Guin will help us understand why turning to imagination should take precedence over an exclusive focus on reality.[3]

2.1 Ghosh's *The Great Derangement*: Imagination vs the Modern Invention of the Real

In *The Great Derangement. Climate Change and the Unthinkable*, Ghosh argues that the ecological crisis is a crisis of imagination (2016:15). Indeed

---

[3] Literature on approaches to ecology via imaginative art and literature is far too abundant to be covered here. For an overview see Buell (1996) and Villanueva-Romero, Kerslake, and Flys-Junquera (2021).

our Western imaginations are obsessed with solitary Promethean destinies, space flights, sanitized environment, smooth and shiny surfaces, and virtual reality. Such constructs lead our imaginations to be the principal drivers of the carbon economy and we seem to have lost the ability to imagine freely. Therefore, says Ghosh, we need to change the matrix altogether – namely, the models and imagining patterns through which any experience is interpreted – and Ghosh points to novels about collective destinies, large time scales, ecosystems' and animals' perspectives, such as Melville's *Moby Dick* or Mallabarman's *A River Called Titash*.

More radically and in line with deep ecological approaches, Ghosh contends that our ecological collective failure results from nothing less than the formation of the idea of the real: A systematic and all-infectious worldview that pre-shapes every possible apprehension of the world and thus literally *constitutes* what we simply see as the real. The same realistic patterns can be found in all cultural expressions, whether in politics, science, or art and literature, but, as Ghosh points out, art and literature especially play a crucial role in revealing these sources of reality, which are in fact imaginative. Ghosh thus shows how the modern novel has nurtured the obsession with reality.

The realist novel is indeed a literary form that has not existed forever. It developed during the seventeenth century, first by showing its contempt for premodern fictions that were too fanciful and quixotic. Characterized as a literary genre, realism now clearly appears as a stylistic effect, a figment of the human imagination clothed in the garb of seriousness. Ghosh provides us with a behind-the-the-scenes look on the great invention of "the real," which is precisely what he also calls "the great derangement."

According to Ghosh, the modern novel is rooted in three major choices, which are the work of the creative imagination, and find their simultaneous expression in supposedly more serious gateways to reality: Science and politics.

First, the modern novel results from a careful selection of "moderate" events. It stages "the orderly bourgeois world" (Ghosh 2016:26) and thus fails to express climatic catastrophes and the uncontrollable forces of nature. The cataclysms we witness today with the climate crisis, which seem to emerge suddenly and elude scientific forecasts, do not fit well into the modern novel. They introduce implausibility, challenging the reader's suspension of disbelief and shifting the novel toward fantasy. Realism emerged alongside rationalism, which assumes that reality has a logical and clear structure, making predictions possible. In line with this perspective, modern sciences assume that change occurs incrementally. In other words, they state we can trace seemingly chaotic events to ordered causal chains. Nonsense, replies Ghosh (2016:25), stressing the growing relevance of non-linearity in today's sciences[4]: Nature does leap. Climate science, geology, and evolutionary biology recognize tipping points and thresholds that lead to alternating periods of stasis, punctuated by short, rapid bursts of catastrophic change that defy simple predictions. The concept of the Anthropocene also highlights how human activity has caused swift, unprecedented environmental changes, where acceleration and escalation are always possible.

The second choice that governs the advent of the modern novel is an anthropocentric definition of the world. This follows from the modern obsession with reality: As Le Guin (2007:87) puts it, realistic fiction is "relentlessly focused on human behavior and psychology." As soon as a novel "begins to include the Other," it becomes outlandish and teeters on the edge of fantasy. Woolf's *Flush* and Melville's *Moby Dick* thus leave an uncanny feeling and encroach on the genre of ghost stories and fables. How would the author know what dogs really think? When a dog is the narrator of a novel, the leap of imagination required is precisely the breach in the orderly bourgeois world that Ghosh describes as unrealistic. Mysterious emotions, interests, and perceptions are alternative sources that can define and shape what is called *the real world*. The rules of literary realism reveal that, through realism, the human has closed itself off from the nonhuman, which is precisely a second root of the great derangement Ghosh describes. These other worlds are ruptures and cracks in the well-ordered, predictable world required to create an effect of reality, and modernity regards the imagination of these worlds as superficial and non-serious.

The third principle of the realist novel is its exclusive interest in the *description* of the world and what Ghosh (2016:80) portrays as "the individual moral adventure." Specifically, the modern novel is the staging of a human subject whose sole field of existence is psychological. This excludes two things: Effective actions and collective beings. For the realist, *the world being and remaining what it is*, each individual can embark on the adventure of her own personal formation, through illusions and disillusions, but there is no question of changing the world. The imagination that constitutes the world is denied in favor of imagination as pure mental representation, and fiction is sidelined in favor of portraying personal adjustments between the mind and external reality. In this view, action is individual, occurring within an unyielding reality, and the minor misadventures of a character are disconnected from the creation of new worlds or the imagination of alternative possibilities.

---

[4] See in particular Gould (1987).

Ghosh (2016:131–3) establishes an essential connection between the individual moral adventure, key to realism in the modern novel, and the ossification of the modern and contemporary political imagination around individual life choices. "You are an environment activist and you use an iPhone, how do you cope with this inconsistency?" Current public policy often takes the form of an appeal to individual responsibility: What can you do daily to protect the planet? Consume less water, buy recycled tote bags and glass bottles? The activists are well aware that collective action, a change that involves the entire social structure, from public policy to large international corporations, is necessary and should be at the heart of the solution, but here again the structure imposed on them by reality as it has been shaped is that of a bundle of individual requests addressed to a political authority or a mysterious set of actors that remain free not to listen. The myth of realism enforced by the modern novel thus appears as a secret key to more "serious" registers of existence, such as politics and activism, that are officially in charge of a direct relationship with reality. This revelation explains the seemingly surprising paradox: a serious relationship with reality *de facto* consists of a psychologization of action and an absence of effective power on reality.

In summary, the real such as created through the invention of realism in the realist novel is in fact a bold fiction. When the modern novel, together with the predominant Western worldview, expresses a raging disdain for fiction – serious writers do not write about witches and orcs – it simply covers up its tracks and enforces its own constructs.

2.2 Le Guin's Praise for Fantasy: Imagining as an Intrinsic End

According to Ghosh, it is a matter of resurrecting the human imagination. A similar injunction can be found in Le Guin's "The Critics, the Monsters, and the Fantasists" (2007). It is worth noting the kinship of this position with the philosophies developed by Derrida and Haraway, who both assign imagination a decisive role in shaping what is called "real" and in instigating the transition to an alternative world.

Ghosh's and Le Guin's praise of imagination is radical in that the call to imagine more in the face of the climate crisis is not just an indication of the means to be employed, but also provides a definition of content and goal. It is not a question of imagining in order to gain better access to true reality, but of getting out of the quest for true reality and exiting "the reality trap" (Le Guin 2007:87). At first, Ghosh's and Le Guin's stance takes us aback: We have to relearn to imagine, very well, but *what* should we imagine? Le Guin speaks out against the way critics often analyze her novels by extracting the moral from them. She does not claim to deliver a set of lessons that could inspire our relationship with today's world and, overall, for Le Guin, the fantasy genre is not meant to provide ready-made morals, rules, and actions to be imitated and transposed into the real world. "Imagine!" if we are to take the call seriously, cannot define in advance what we ought to imagine. However, if we take a closer look, it is not an injunction that leaves us completely clueless about the change at stake.

In Le Guin's view, the function of the fantasy genre is to open up to the world of the Other-than-human. When we read *The Lord of the Rings*, we are thrown into a world worthy of the name, whose paths and potentialities remain to be explored. It is the premodern, pre-industrial world where children feel "at home" (Le Guin 2007:87) – a world they attend to with amazement and fear as they discover their surroundings. They play in the garden, the forest, or the nearby streets, wondering what they might find beyond the hill or behind the distant palisade. They imagine following a column of ants into the maze of underground corridors, a familiar yet mysterious universe. Fantasy unveils a vast land with endless horizons, where billions of different species – potential partners or foes – coexist. While Ghosh emphasizes the importance of imagining alternative possibilities, Le Guin demonstrates that thinking in terms of possibilities is already an achievement, as it opens us up not to a fictional world, but to the larger world as the realm of otherness.

To clarify this, let us first stress that, in essence, imagination operates holistically, moving from the whole to the parts – unlike analytical or rational thinking. If I ask you to imagine a dragon, I am not expecting you to define the premises or specifications from which you want to start, nor to draw up a list of clear, well-understood principles and definitions as the basis for a series of deductions. To imagine is to conjure an image, namely a concrete presence. This image arises carrying with it a whole texture of intertwined aspects and components that you can analyze ad infinitum, but that first envelops and absorbs you. An image is a strange flesh that initially surprises us and affects us emotionally. Similarly, to read a novel is to be transported into a slice of existence inseparable from an emerging world, one that comes with all the depth of its horizons, emotional tones, and atmospheres – an overall effect that cannot be reduced to specific words or aspects in the text. This holistic perspective is crucial to developing a relationship with the world around us that is open to its strangeness. The whole surpasses and submerges us; it frightens us as much as it invites us to explore it infinitely and cautiously. This is how other-than-human perspectives and interests touch us, as both different from ours and integral to the world that sustains us, outside which we are nothing. Because imagination is the ability to think holistically rather than analytically – through figures, images, metaphors, and schemata – it is indispensable for understanding milieus and the world as wholes.

In this new light, Ghosh's analyses gain even more radical significance: Calling for imagination is essentially calling for opening ourselves up to the unsettling and amazing genuine *experience* of precariousness, unpredictability, collectives, and the nonhuman. Imagination, embodied and concrete in contrast to theoretical thinking, is the terrain on which I can make experiences while the pressure of the myth of reality is removed. This way, I can acquire new skills to interact with the aspects of the world obscured by realism and incorporate them into my field of action.

In a sense, it is a matter of returning to the romance, the literary form that preceded the modern novel, where strangeness still had its rightful place and could proliferate freely. Ghosh (2016:159) thus refers us to a vision that is "at once new and ancient." This formulation merits attention as it allows us to reject a realistic interpretation of Ghosh's position. What do we find when we open ourselves to the greater world? First, a literary form that does not care to pursue the "true reality." Second, a world that is open to interpretations and changes with them. Since the development of the modern novel – inseparable from profound social and technological upheaval – the world has changed, proving that it is not an invariable natural backdrop, that is, a reality that endures while the ideas and works that represent it pass away. Instead, it is an open-ended, ambiguous entity that fluctuates between actual realizations and countless possibilities, remaining in the ontological realm of the unresolved: Nothing is entirely what it appears to be. It is precisely for this reason that imagination should prevail today – rather than a return to a forgotten reality – as climate change presents humanity with unprecedented challenges.

According to Le Guin, the fantasy genre tells us: Go out into the world, explore, be open to all those other beings – trolls, dragons, orcs – walk the paths, expose yourself to what scares and amazes you. Leave your home as Frodo did when he went out on the road in *The Lord of the Rings* and expect to discover a thousand lands. It is a challenge worth taking seriously because it has the power to effectively change our attitude and the world as we constitute it.

There is no doubt that Ghosh and Le Guin confront us with the "other world" that activists invoke, namely, both Gaia as a whole, endowed with its own tendencies and meanings, and a new paradigm that could entirely dismantle the foundations of the modern world, which is grounded in the denial of Gaia. They offer us nothing less than a radical revolution in paradigms, providing a method for reimagining the world. However, for Ghosh and Le Guin, everything hinges on the way we represent the world to ourselves. Admittedly, this representation is never a sheer mental picture. It involves an attitude and a way of constituting the world that rely on collective institutions and also permeate our actions and the works we produce, affecting the earth itself. In this sense, Le Guin (2007:86) highlights that "A literal mind is a great asset to reading fantasy." Yet she immediately qualifies this statement: "but not when it has been programmed too rigidly." And indeed, ultimately, for Le Guin, the key is not in the alliance between literality and realism, but in the imagination of a completely different world, because a world not dominated by the human is *elsewhere*.

Here we find ourselves at a significant critical point, where two tendencies come into tension. Ghosh and Le Guin want to change the matrix, namely, the very framework of imagination that shapes the world. But their works engage us as individuals who, first and foremost, forge a certain representation of the world. Hence some paradoxical ethicizing formulas in *The Great Derangement* that clash with Ghosh criticism of the model of the individual moral adventure. For instance, Ghosh (2016:133) calls to our imagination and the imagination of artists and writers: "When future generations look back upon the Great Derangement they will certainly blame the leaders and politicians of this time for their failure to address the climate crisis. But they may well hold artists and writers equally culpable – for *the imagining of possibilities* is not, after all, the job of politicians and bureaucrats." Everyone is urged to learn to imagine differently and to imagine a wholly different world. Le Guin and Ghosh thus emphasize what comes across as a theoretical utopia: Let us imagine a completely different world. However, the very idea of representation and utopian imagination is profoundly anthropocentric: The modern humans dream of themselves as visionaries, free imaginations that shape the world, but they remain animals caught up in their desires, interests, passions, and power relations. Don't we have to get rid of the idea that we are working on ideas and fantasies? Don't we need to *exit the matrix* instead of simply trying to *change matrices* and substituting just another worldview to the Anthropocentric modern one?

3 Calling for More Realism

In *Ecocriticism on the Edge*, Timothy Clark (2015:196) warns against the environmental humanities' tendency to "[overinvest] in the power of cultural representations, of the social importance of art and literature." Ecocritics "repeatedly refer to the 'social imaginary' or the 'cultural imaginary' as their object of engagement" (Clark 2015:18). However, Clark argues, at a time when concrete changes are urgently needed, "to exaggerate the importance of the imaginary is, in itself, to run the risk of consolidating a kind of diversionary side-show, blind to its relative insignificance" (21). Yet, from the beginning, environmental studies have been shaped by a call for realism, driven by an ecological crisis that challenges anthropocentrism. This perspective indeed directs us toward a pre-human, physicochemical, and geological reality that transcends our human viewpoint. Taking the argument further, a realist approach contrasts with relying on imagination to address the climate crisis, instead criticizing human imagination as one of the causes of this crisis.

In contemporary environmental studies, the plea for salvation through imagination thus coexists with an equally strong call for environmental realism. Strangely, these two views rarely confront each other directly. Instead, authors tend to choose one side, oscillate between them, or implicitly combine both without addressing the inherent tensions.

The following is a brief examination of the realist solution as put forth by several of its key proponents. The authors I will mention are linked by common theses and influences and they are assertively the heirs of Nietzsche and Kafka. This environmental realism is rooted in a will to act instead of representing and depicting. It re-anchors texts and individuals in their concrete and bodily situation. In this way, on many occasions, it expresses an aversion to the figurative mode of speech, and, by extension, to symbolic systems in general.

One of the precursors of this trend and a key figure in environmental humanities, French philosopher Gilles Deleuze (1994:129) analyzes Western thinking as humanity's creation of an "image of thought." He argues this "image" reflects the belief that we perceive the world as something external to us, which we can observe, represent, and describe through various means such as paintings, philosophical works, and other forms of expression (8, 301). We trust we are facing the world, capturing its essence *through* these re-presentations, while, in reality, we are irrevocably entangled within the world. Even those who believe that they stand in the theoretical realm of contemplation and abstract knowledge are in fact made of flesh, emotions, and habits that remain embedded in the network of the actual environment, and so are their words and ideas: Sheer reality through and through. In other words, they are actors rather than thinkers. Let us examine how realism and ecological concerns become closely intertwined in the work of Coetzee, Adams, Norris, and Diamond.

3.1 Realism and Environmental Activism in Coetzee's Elisabeth Costello

Elisabeth Costello, an aging novelist, is invited to give an academic lecture at Appelton College as a celebrated author. During the event, she subverts expectations by delivering a disjointed and intentionally uncomfortable discourse on animal suffering. The situation becomes even more incongruous when Costello, referencing Kafka's short story "Report to an Academy," claims that she feels somewhat like Red Peter, the ape who has become human-like, in front of her audience, asserting that there is no irony in this statement (Coetzee 2003:49–50). Costello aims to express things *as they are* and to reach "the thing itself, the only thing" (167). She insists, "I have a literal cast of mind" (60), after claiming to channel Red Peter's voice (54). The book plays devilishly with reminding the reader that words are illusions (17) and that the story being told is fiction – for instance Costello is Coetzee's doppelgänger and yet not really him. But ultimately, precisely through moments of brutal honesty, the novel produces a shock of realism in the reader. Coetzee cunningly passes the Good News along: The author is no longer lying; he is not creating an image of reality. "The word-mirror is broken, irreparably" (17). Accordingly, Costello emphasizes Kafka as a realist author (16–7, 27) and argues that, in his poem *The Jaguar*, Ted Hughes does not merely depict a jaguar but allows the reader to "be, for a brief while, the jaguar" (77).

In what way does this effort toward realism serve an ecological purpose? Coetzee's *Elisabeth Costello* is haunted by the question of ecological *activism*. Costello is appalled that most people manage to live alongside animal suffering as if it were nothing. There is an urgent need to act, and Costello makes it her mission to convince her audience through shock therapy. The arguments she uses are often fanciful and sloppy – "she's rambling," remarks repeatedly her philosopher daughter-in-law (Coetzee 2003:59) – and her speech is a mixture of loose philosophical analysis, pathos, and performance. This is in fact a deliberate strategy, for Costello believes that the root of the problem lies precisely in our ability to obscure reality with a web of fancy and heartless reasonings (62).

Building on this, Costello advocates for a holistic approach to animal protection, in a typically deep-ecological fashion, but in a way that leads to a path quite different from that developed by Le Guin and Ghosh. "To thinking, cogitation, I oppose fullness, embodiedness, the sensation of (. . .) being alive to the world. This fullness contrasts starkly with Descartes' key state, which has an empty feel to it: The feel of a pea rattling around in a shell" (Coetzee 2003:61–2). What makes Kafka a realist according to Costello is that he is putting us back at the very heart of our animality and the harshest experience of our physicality and "embeddedness" (27). Costello argues that Kafka's portrayal of the ape, Red Peter, is "embedded" in two significant ways. First, Kafka refuses to romanticize Red Peter's experience: "That ape is followed through to the end, to the bitter, unsayable end" (27). Second, Kafka and the reader are contaminated by Red Peter's experience. Unlike rationalists, who view Kafka's fables and allegories as mere metaphors disconnected from our true nature, Costello contends that Kafka's depiction reflects our genuine condition: "[Kafka's] ape is embedded as we are embedded, you in me, I in you" (27). One of Costello's key claims is that humans do indeed experience animal suffering, and that its reality profoundly and indisputably impacts us (61–3). In her view, to suggest that this experience is merely imaginary is both inaccurate and morally unacceptable.

3.2 Carol Adams: Metaphors and the Denial of Real Animals

In many ways, Costello is close to Carol Adams, who formulates several clear arguments for a realist position in *The Sexual Politics of Meat*. Adams, too, locates her work primarily in the realm of activism and would prefer not to call it *academic* (Adams 1990:14). This positioning points to the prevailing tendency in the Western world to install academic thought in a theoretical bubble: "Activists don't just imagine that world [without animal cruelty]. We work to bring the world we imagine into existence. Join us" (7).

For Adams (1990:72), activism has everything to do with the way we should use words: Literally, not metaphorically. Indeed, Adams explains how "a metaphoric system of Language" (67) prevents us from fully acknowledging the reality of animal suffering. The use of metaphor thus contributes to the invisibilization and alienation of nonhuman animals. For example, victims of sexual assault often say "I felt like meat," a troubling metaphor that expresses a visceral and, as Adams acknowledges, meaningful feeling (81–4). The victims sense a deep kinship between the exploitation of nonhuman animals and patriarchal structural sexism, a kinship Carol Adams is keen to highlight, but as a reality, not a metaphor. Adams is highly critical of such metaphors because they obfuscate the reality of both experiences: That of the victims of sexual assault and that of the nonhuman animals who are *literally* turned into dead meat. "Feminists among others, appropriate the metaphor of butchering without acknowledging the originating oppression of animals that generates the power of the metaphor. (...), Western culture constantly renders the material reality of violence into controlled and controllable metaphors" (68). Therefore "what is absent from much feminist theory that relies on metaphors of animals' oppression for illuminating women's experience is the reality behind the metaphor" (90).

To be precise, Adams suggests that the problem lies not in the phrase "feeling like meat," but in our spontaneous tendency to understand it as a figurative way of speaking. This tendency leads to an impasse: The phrase is paradoxical – meat is dead, how could it feel? – and takes us beyond the realm of words, into what cannot be logically and fully thought out. We try to transpose ourselves into meat *in imagination*, while at the same time admitting that this transposition is literally impossible and can only be achieved with empty words (Adams 1990:67). Adams thus suggests that "metaphor itself" may be "the very undergarment to the garb of oppression" (73), critiquing not just individual metaphors but the entire symbolic system of language, which makes each thing exist "only through what it represents." Metaphorization – the displacement of meaning (from the Greek meta, "beyond," and pherein, "to carry") and indirect representation – is indeed inherent in symbolic systems, as they attempt to represent reality through words.

3.3 Realism and the Return to Bodies, Powers, and Acts

A recurring thesis in the environmental realist-activist movement is the rejection of language as mimesis – the idea that language merely reflects reality and is a symbolic system whose function is to represent the real. This stance challenges realism as a literary device that creates an *effect* of reality while remaining stuck in representational and artificial mediations. Instead, it advocates for a more radical, metaphysical realism: the commitment to opening to reality itself. To be sure, once the tricks of mimesis are unmasked, one of the remaining paths is relativism accompanied by contempt for that daydream that humans have long called "knowledge" (Nietzsche 2020:119). But there is a way to save realism by reminding us that words are also material bodies and forces of action: effective realities.

Coetzee thus insists on the physical power of words: Costello writes with an insight that "shakes" her son (Coetzee 2003:6); she develops a "heated rather than cool" (52) way of speaking and does not hesitate to use "tasteless" examples and comparisons – such as the comparison between the exploitation of animals and the Holocaust – knowing full well that she will jar her audience. She is interested in words that are like a shock, like electricity (87, 139). She is "cruel" (6), her son John notes, and has evolved into a cat writer, "one of those large cats that pause as they eviscerate their victim and, across the torn-open belly, give you a cold yellow stare." Derek Attridge (2004:654) thus establishes a fundamental connection between Coetzee's oeuvre, literal reading, and what he calls "the literature in the event" which defines writing and reading processes as events that *occur* rather than as "a theme to be registered, a thesis to be grasped, or an imperative to be followed or ignored": Coetzee's literary work conveys the ethical experience that makes us engage in reading and writing as performance in action.

Carol Adams goes even further, showing that the violence done to animals really begins in the *performative* power of metaphor (Adams 1990:66–7). Adams argues that the symbolic use of language creates absent referents: The word takes center stage, while the reality that gave flesh to its meaning fades and disappears. This reality is replaced by a theoretical, manipulable meaning, reassuring to the human speaker. Any approach to language as a symbolic system involves the creation of absent referents. What sets Adams' theory apart is her emphasis on the role of animal exploitation in this process. We create new words [e.g. roast, chop, sausage, bacon] to designate the animal transformed into meat, to make people forget that this steak is a burnt corpse. We refer to animals extensively in all kinds of imaginative uses of language and to describe and represent human emotions or character traits. At first sight, Adams seems to leave the exact nature of the articulation between the processing of animals into symbols and the mass slaughter of animals for human consumption in the shadows. One could be the cause or symbol of the other for instance. In fact, Adams suggests the absence of distance between these two phenomena. Both are equally real and performative, *they go hand in hand*. The separation of the animal from its living reality by dissolving it into words and metaphors is the necessary condition that enables slaughter without a crisis of conscience. The metaphorization is already a *real* separation and the killing is the bloody end of its realization. It thus appears that symbolic language and the process of mimesis *are in fact* a butchery that cuts reality into *literal* slices.

3.4 Realism and Becoming Animal

As Margot Norris demonstrates in *Beasts of the Modern Imagination* (1985:1), the movement centered around literality and realism, with Nietzsche and Kafka as its two leading figures, can be characterized as biocentric. Costello also highlights this idea, using it to clarify the statement "The word-mirror is broken." She continues: "About what is really going on in the lecture hall your guess is as good as mine: men and men, men and apes, apes and men, apes and apes. The lecture hall itself may be nothing but a zoo" (Coetzee 2003:17). Indeed, humans easily forget that words are bodies, with their own music and texture, and that orderly reality is a precarious bourgeois construct. Humans have established relatively stable symbolic systems, which leads to the mistaken belief that words transparently connect our minds to reality. The zoo Costello mentions signals the rediscovery of the animalistic nature of human language, seen here as a contingent, evolving technique through which species – including humans – creatively shape their world. Words are thus understood as expressions of life within a framework of negotiation that mirrors the interests, desires, whims, idiosyncrasies, and power dynamics among various living beings. Consequently, words appear as opaque and treacherous. Accordingly, Kafka explodes any possibility of making sense of the world through symbolic systems. Not only are the themes of music, the ineffable, and the illogical central to his work, but his books are also machines for dissolving language, revealing it as a series of trapdoors and a devious, dangerous nest of forces (Norris 1985:133).

The critical difference here is between language as being *about* reality (and therefore doomed to miss it, insofar as it is the matrix of all-too-human images and mediations) and language *as a reality*, on the same level as living bodies, fangs, tools, seductive displays, or luring behaviors. Costello thus considers that Hughes' poem "is not about the animal, but is instead the record of an engagement with him" (Coetzee 2003:75). This notion of a "record" echoes a thesis by Hofmannsthal (1979:72) – a key reference for Coetzee – in "The Poet ad This Time": Poems function like a seismograph, not describing objects, but reverberating physical impacts.

This ties into Costello's concept of embeddedness: We are enmeshed in the material world, and animal suffering resonates in all the fibers of our bodies, regardless of our lack of words to describe it.

But while Costello still refers to a process of "imagining our way into [the jaguar's] way of moving," Deleuze (1988:232), also an inheritor of Nietzsche and Kafka, and the philosopher who theorized the most thoroughly the critique of mimesis, is adamant to do away with any reference to the imagination of what animals experience, preferring to speak of "becoming-animal." What is accomplished in becomings-animal is – also sometimes due to the impact of our encounter with words, their rhythms, and their unique effectiveness – a change in the style in which our behavior, our tastes, and our metabolism develop. Becomings-animal have nothing to do with a fantasy or an imitation, they are processes that take place in every particle of our body and function more like a virus infection (238).

David Abram, another prominent contemporary theorist of animal becoming, manages in a more nuanced way than Deleuze to combine a realist position with the call to transport ourselves into the lived experience of animals. His analysis thus fleshes out a thesis that Costello outlines but does not fully substantiate. Unlike Deleuze, Abram attaches great importance to the lived dimension of becoming-animal, describing it as a veritable merging: Suddenly we become the nonhuman other and see the world through her eyes. For Costello, as for Abram, empathy is a real leap into the world of an animal, hence Abram's realist stance: Becoming animal is not a metaphor or a fantasy, it is a real metamorphosis that brutally carries us away into a "gleaming, glistening world without people" (Abram 2011:229). Abram indeed employs the classic rhetoric of the clash between human understanding and a mysterious and obdurate reality. Becoming animal, a "perfectly impossible" (203) event, leaves us shocked and speechless, unfolding as a breakaway under the shaman's direction, without the subject fully understanding it. Abram views this transformation as occurring at the level of sensations and perceptions, which he characterizes as "immediate" (90, 223) and raw contact with the world, as opposed to articulated thought, explanations (201), and sense: "I understood nothing of what [the shaman] said, and had no need to" (217). And indeed, the final aspect of Abram's realism that resonates with Costello's is that becoming animal is achieved exclusively through body-centered practices. Abram describes the patient bodily exercises performed by the shaman that enable metamorphosis:

> To move as another is simply the most visceral approach to feel one's way into the body of that creature, and so to taste the flavor of its experience, entering into the felt intelligence of the other. [...] Merely calling to the creature in one's imagination will never suffice; one must summon it bodily, entering mimetically into the shape and rhythm of the other being if the animal spirit is to feel the call. One must unbind the human arrangement of one's senses, and those of any humans watching, if the animal is to feel safe enough to arrive in our midst. (213–4)

Like Costello, Abram explicitly links this radical empathy to the search for a new ontological and social model that can completely transform our relationship with the earth. "In a crisis-ridden world" and for a civilization that has lost touch with its animal nature and replaced it with theoretical constructs, "our greatest hope for the future" (Abram 2011:246) rests in the body's faith in (246) – or empathy with (271) – the surrounding terrain (271) that sustains us. Becoming animal is precisely the way we can reconnect with this "immediate experience" of the "land that enfolds us" (89–90). Empathic fusion, Abram contends, also converts us into a nonhuman animal experience that he defines as a holistic relation to everything around, "a carnal realm wherein my animal body was engaged in this ongoing interchange with the animate earth" (201). When the magical metamorphosis occurs, Abrams feels "far more palpably present, and real, to the rocks and the shadowed cliffs than [he]'d felt before." He even feels "that [he is] known to these mountains now. (...). Every facet of the world is awake, and you within it" (201). Interestingly the conversion to a holistic perspective is here enforced under the banner of realism, in other words, it is less an imaginative worldview than a new praxis. Without doubt, this conceptualization also does greater justice to the realist perspective that Costello aims to establish.

3.5 Diamond's Reading of Coetzee and a New Realism

Doing justice to Coetzee's *The Lives of Animals* as the embodiment of a genuine realism is precisely the task Cora Diamond (2008) sets herself in "The Difficulty of Reality and the Difficulty of Philosophy." In line with the heirs of Nietzsche and Kafka I mentioned earlier, Diamond contrasts human thought with reality. In her view, it is a mistake to read Coetzee's book as a series of arguments about animal rights, as Peter Singer and Barbara Smut do (48–9). The strength of Costello's discourse lies precisely in the fact that it is not a discourse about "ideas" that "can be extracted and examined" (49) – a representational approach to animals – but rather "the presenting" (49) of a "wounded" animal before our eyes (46–7). Costello is "marked" and isolated by the holocaust of nonhuman animals and her empathizing with the death of animals. Of course, the rationalist argues that we cannot think of death and simultaneously have direct access to the reality of death, but Coetzee's text is the embodiment of the unspeakable unease that sometimes seizes us and makes us feel, beyond all logic, the abyss that death is. It is an unthinkable knowledge that we experience in the raw: A "knowledge that we are" (Diamond 2008:73, Coetzee 2003:60–1).

Diamond emphatically connects becoming-a-wounded-animal to genuine realism. To establish this link, she coins an original definition of the latter: She defines reality as that which is experienced as the "difficulty of reality" (Diamond 2008:45). Reality "resists" our efforts to think it, or, possibly, is "taken to be painful in its inexplicability" (45–6); it does not lend itself to the demands for clarity and perfect understanding that are the expression of a fallacious bourgeois realism. The orderly bourgeois alleged "reality" resists so little, in fact, that it does not deserve the name of reality; it must be a view of the mind. Diamond (1991) also rejects classical metaphysical realism, which claims that reality is entirely outside the realm of our thoughts. Reality, in her view, functions as that which tantalizes us, and accordingly Diamond defines human efforts at representation and argumentation – the general enterprise she calls "philosophy" – as a means of *deflecting reality* (Diamond 2008:58–60). Diamond concludes even more radically by stressing that the "coming apart of thought and reality belongs to flesh and bones" (78). The only way to approach reality in the human realm of thought is through failure and frustration, a typically realist assertion.

Accordingly, Diamond explains Costello's strategy as a way of embodying "knowledge" through "a terrible rawness of nerves" (Diamond 2008:47). In Diamond's words, this knowledge that we *are* is the experience of a contradiction, a conceptual impossibility (62) that hurts us, "shoulders language out from the game" (45) and "shoulders one out of how one thinks" (58).

To summarize, we have encountered three realisms. (1) Literary realism, as a stylistic effect, is the exact opposite of an openness to reality worthy of the name, in all its savagery and inhumanity. (2) Metaphysical realism enjoins us to aim for the real beyond human symbols and representations. (3) And, the "realistic spirit" open to the "difficulties of reality" in Diamond's theory seems to me to be a variant of the metaphysical realism, but recognizes that reality is not completely cut off from any relation to human thought. It nevertheless defines this relation in terms of an infinite quest, violence, and even impossibility. Here the conflict between this realist trend and the approach discussed in the previous section, exemplified by the work of Le Guin and Ghosh, comes fully to light. The dividing line lies between a radical distrust *or* a fundamental confidence in the imagination and, correlatively, between the reference *or* absence of reference to a reality that contradicts the symbolic register and therefore highjacks literature, violates, frustrates, and dismantles it.

4 A Destructive Debate

The tension between realism and imagination is central to understanding today's ecological crisis, but it is also an integral part of the crisis itself, intensifying rather than resolving it. The aporias in two important works on these themes, those of Coetzee and Latour, reveal this tension, along with the high risk of powerlessness it entails.

4.1 Elizabeth Costello's Despair: Caught in the Imagination-Reality Loop

Elizabeth Costello begins with realism and ends in the most baroque allegory (Klopper 2008:120). "At the gate," the final section of the book, offers a pastiche of Kafka's stories and shows Costello at the end of her journey, where she finds herself in an undetermined place, and summoned by an obscure gatekeeper to make a statement of belief, failing which she will not be allowed to continue on her way. The ordeal drags on: Unable to provide any satisfactory answer, she is repeatedly questioned and evaluated by a panel of judges, revealing that the realism she advocated in the first part of the book cannot withstand the test.

"I am a writer," Costello initially responds, "it is not my profession to believe, just to write. [...] I do imitations as Aristotle would have said" (Coetzee 2003:149). As a "trader in fiction" (150), Costello is tasked with having no beliefs herself. She attempts to defend herself against the judges' reluctance to give credit to her statement by claiming that she is a "secretary of the invisible" and a spokesperson for different perspectives. Each morning she prepares for the summons from what she calls "voices" (157) and "powers beyond us" (154). Her statement takes a boastful and increasingly idealistic turn when she irritably declares that these voices are all legitimate in dictating books to her, provided they "speak the truth" (157). "How can you be so sure? Are these voices coming from God?" The judges ask, before Costello falls into silence, overwhelmed by a violent headache.

Throughout the book, bursts of idealism – hopes of redemption through an absolute power far removed from human finitude and accessed via allegories and imaginative surges – alternate with violent returns to the harsh reality of the suffering, aging body, eventually giving way to a sense of bafflement. "Confused" is the jury's verdict (170), as Costello's coherence dissolves.

In fact, Coetzee does not really help us examine new solutions to the dilemma facing animal right activists and environmental activists. Instead, he raises this dilemma to a paroxysm of sophistication, showing its ancient roots and staging the process through which the debate gets stuck in a loop. Both imaginative idealist upsurges and returns to realism are sincere, yet this montage in the form of a dead-end dialogue at crossed purposes is in fact a classic of modernity. Coetzee somehow spills the beans by paying tribute to Hofmannsthal's *Letter of Lord Chandos* (2008) – a masterpiece of overindulgent modern existential crisis – as an afterword to *Elizabeth Costello*. This letter of Lord Chandos is key to understanding why environmental studies must overcome the tension between realism and imaginarism.

The letter of Lord Chandos creates an effect of reality within fiction: Lord Chandos – Hofmannsthal's fictional doppelgänger – a once prolific writer of the lyrical, idealist genre, addresses a letter to a real figure, his contemporary Francis Bacon, to announce his retirement from literature. At issue is an existential crisis he faces, which he believes is due to an incompatibility between, on the one hand hyper-detailed holistic visions, where he truly merges with other perspectives and feels the resonance of all interactions among living beings and their environment, and, on the other hand, the limitations of language, which is always too poor and fragmented.

Elizabeth Costello turns into Elizabeth Chandos, and writes her own letter to Francis Bacon. "We cannot live thus" (Coetzee 2003:175), she repeats: The revelations that grip her husband and render him speechless drive him away from her. "We are not made for revelation," as revelation belongs to the time of giants and angels, whereas, for now, it is the time of fleas. Here Costello, as so often, expresses a voice of realism. However, the bottom line is that Lord and Lady C., Hofmannsthal and Coetzee, are saying the same thing: A superabundance of reality lies beyond us and eludes human language and symbols, placing both the writer and humanity in a tension between impossible quest and disappointed renunciation.

Lord Chandos' letter is, depending on how you read it, both a pinnacle of modern poetry and a farce. And indeed, Coetzee and Hofmannsthal perform the same trick: They write to say that it is impossible to write. Page after page, they describe difficulties that their books largely overcome in practice. Thus, Coetzee reminds us of our ability to empathize with the suffering of animals and of the possibility of transposing ourselves into another, and Chandos describes in vivid detail his supposedly "unspeakable" visions. Chandos renounces literature, while Hofmannsthal plays a clever double game. For Hofmannsthal, the gain is clearly in finally being the hero who succeeds in speaking the unspeakable. By dramatizing Chandos' difficulties, he creates the impressive figure of a radical reality that lies outside words and is alien to human thought – in short, *reality* in the radically realist sense of the word. And because Hofmannsthal describes what Chandos feels but cannot express, he achieves what the modern novel always strives for: The true expression of *the real real*.

I suspect that Coetzee is resorting to the same trick as Hofmannsthal. Costello is indeed a new Chandos: Tired, in crisis, vacillating between great moments of holistic enthusiasm and a disenchanted materialism. She is also a bit of a poser, as she sometimes admits. Coetzee treats her with a mixture of sympathy and derision, but, like her, he vacillates between allegorical imagination and a desire for more realism, between the raw, often ugly and disgusting, body and the need for meaning and understanding that haunts the human spirit. Coetzee plays with, dramatizes, but hardly deconstructs these questionable dichotomies.

Diamond falls into the same pattern when she insists on the connection between what she calls the difficulties of the real and Coetzee's descriptions of the challenge of grasping what it is like to be a bat or a corpse. Diamond sees right through Coetzee's charades: A part of Coetzee's plan is indeed to reach the real via the Chandossian way, that of "difficulties." The more difficulties one encounters, Diamond points out, the more one opens to reality. Yet Diamond's approach misses another aspect of Coetzee's text, to wit the postmodern crisis that keeps returning to excruciating doubts regarding the ability of saying anything that is not a mere construct of reality, a make-believe, and a posture. Diamond's whole point is to make sense of this doubt as a last resort: Because the writer is going through so much doubt and is so disturbed by what he is trying in vain to say, we can be sure he is confronting the difficulties of reality instead of retreating into habitual, reassuring patterns of thought. Diamond seems to forget that it is an old literary trick to stage difficulties to *create an effect of reality*.

The result, much more than the cause, of this Chandossian stance is a significant loss of agency. Both Coetzee and Diamond indeed emphasize powerlessness in front of the difficulties of the real and Elizabeth Costello drowns in increasingly theoretical and confused considerations. Essentialized difficulty becomes an object of fantasy, awe, or lamentations.

4.2 The Impasses of Latour's Ecological Realism

Latour's trajectory is very similar to that of Elizabeth Costello. In many respects, Latour is a new environmental realist, in a complex sense that we will analyze in the following paragraphs.

Admittedly, Latour has done a great deal to overcome classical realism, which views reality as an independent entity separate from human beings. Latour (2019) relentlessly insists that Gaia is not a coordinating Providence. Gaia consists of myriads (micro-) organisms that maintain the atmosphere and enable the propagation of life. Gaia is (are) a multiplicity of unpredictable agents rather than implacable universal laws. There is, Latour emphasizes, no heterogeneity between alleged "natural" and human agents, which is why this distinction must give way to the study of "hybrids" (Latour 1993:1–3), in other words human actions that are born and develop in a determined and limiting material context, as well as earthly processes that intrinsically bear the mark of the Anthropocene.

Accordingly, for many years, Latour elaborated a theory characterized by a central political component: Everything is and will be a matter of negotiation, and we need to "imagine" a peace negotiation between various and often conflicting players, such as wildfires, flooded rivers, the ozone layer, nuclear power plants, politicians, scientists, industry, and international finance (1993:138–145).

I was therefore taken aback the day I heard Latour becoming the most unexpected prophet of the tragedy. In 2020, not only does Latour (2020a: 31'-34') reject a purely relativist approach that would claim Trump and Greta Thunberg both live on equally virtual planets, he also contends that the contemporary situation, characterized by the rebellion of the Earth, has crossed a critical threshold and democracy is no longer an option. We are now in an era he calls the era of "tragedy": The earth, nonhuman animals, seas, and rivers are not *begging us* to give them more rights and a voice in political discussions, they "forced us to bow to something which look like another power." The new normal is that nonhuman beings are putting us under radical pressure: Negotiations are over, Latour argues, and either humans "submit," in a political submission that will be nothing more than a formal recognition of a more fundamental absolute dependence, or they take refuge in denial.

Let us take a closer look at *Facing Gaia* and *Down to Earth* to trace back the emergence of Latour's second-instance realism. Latour (2017:58)[5] indeed frequently asserts his commitment to reality and realism. This affirmation first takes on meaning in contrast to those he calls the moderns who, following Galileo and Descartes, see themselves as detached from their earthly situation. The discovery of universal laws allowed them to know the movements of bodies intellectually, not through the senses. However, as Lovelock showed, this perspective overlooks Earth's uniqueness: The pure mind of modern science would never have a chance to travel freely in imagination throughout the universe if it were not primarily sustained by the distinctive earthly atmosphere and its fragile balance. It would not exist without its entanglement with countless micro-organisms. Latour concludes that "the moderns" are in delusion and claims to unveil reality as it manifests when "we stop pretending" (73).

Latour's realism takes a radical and particularly problematic form in connections to two tendencies: exasperation in the face of climate denial, and an attempt to speak as the prophet of an absolute Revolution.

The following passage reflects the prophetic tone Latour sometimes adopts: "If Gaia could speak, it would say, like Jesus: "Do not suppose that I have come to bring peace to the earth. I did not come to bring peace, but a sword" (Matt. 10:34). Or, more violently still, as in the apocryphal Gospel of Thomas: "I have cast fire upon the world, and behold, I guard it until it is ablaze" (Latour 2017:144). This also reveals Latour's double play: He invokes Gaia as a singular deity with clear, bellicose intentions, while simultaneously holding that there are many agents, not just "one" Gaia. This ambiguity also surfaces when Latour explains that intentionality resides in the various micro-organisms, *not* in Gaia as a whole (99–100). In a bid to dodge charges of irrationality, Latour loses one of Lovelock's and Margulis' key insights: Just as organisms exhibit agency beyond the simple juxtaposition of their parts, Gaia is the emergence of such a precarious unity, multiple yet exceeding the limited perspective of each of its "parts." In this sense, contrary to Latour's claim (98), Gaia is both *a whole* (more precisely: An emerging, unfinished *process of totalization*) *and its parts* (which contribute to the emergence of a general terrestrial dynamic but can act independently or in conflict). Latour oscillates between two equally enigmatic figures of Gaia: The one who speaks to us like Jesus, and the myriad entities "conspiring by sustaining the atmosphere" (97),

---

[5] See also p.242, 245, 257–8, 265, 270 and Latour 2018:36, 37, 39, 55, 59.

a mere "muddle" (100). Latour thus continues to capitalize Gaia and alternates between "She" and "They."

The same ambivalence appears in Latour's tentative concept of the agency of things in *Facing Gaia*. According to Latour, agency in things is defined by scientists through the combination of an analysis of forces – what things do – and the idea of purpose, intentionality, and will. The most daring aspect of Latour's concept of agency is the idea that agency comes from the future, by contrast with causality that tries to encapsulate the destiny of everything in its past (Latour 2017:69). A "thing with agency" acts in a creative way that overflows and defies causal laws. Hence, for instance, the plasticity of the brain or the eye I mentioned earlier. This somewhat existentialist approach to Gaia yet clashes with Latour's realism. As he introduces his concept of agency, Latour starts with Tolstoy's description of General Kutuzov's desperate decision in *War and Peace*, when feeling powerless over the unfolding situation: All that remains is for him to "[give] his approval to the accomplished fact" (50). This rhetorical, deeply ambivalent, formula is quite unfortunately used by Latour as a guide for the rest of the analysis: Agency is the combination of facts and will. However, if it is a fait accompli, there is only an illusory will, and if there is value in assent, there was still a chance, even a minuscule possibility of diverting the fact about to be fulfilled. By contrast, Latour proceeds by aggregating facts and will, in constant leaps, without explaining where exactly the creative agency takes shape. About a set of peptides that are described by a team of scientists to "play important and diverse roles in coordinating endocrine, autonomic, metabolic, and behavioral responses to stress" (55), Latour states: "Having a function is its way of having goals, or in any case of being defined as a vector, and thus as an agent" (55). In other words, if it quite vaguely "plays a role," it must be an agent. Similarly, after defining the agency of rivers, Latour asks: "How can we doubt that the Atchafalaya 'wants to capture' the Mississippi?" (53). The corps fought against this will of the Atchafalaya but Latour quotes one of the engineers: "It is not a question of whether or not the Atchafalaya will end up capturing the entire river, but a question of *when*" (54), thus endorsing the claim that the fate is sealed. In these analyses, Latour consistently proceeds by leaps, from facts to will and back. Where exactly does the ability to invent the future, that is the core of agency, emerge in these hybrids? Latour does not tell us and it is precisely this emergence that we will have to study in the next sections, which will lead us beyond the wobbly association of the accomplished fact and of a mysterious will.

Latour's ambivalent realist rhetoric is explained by the context of the current climate denial situation. In *Down to Earth*, Latour (2018) rightly shows that a social and economic elite sensed very early on the irremediable turn taken by the climate crisis: There will not be enough resources for everyone. Here Latour cleverly interprets climate denial as the covert victory of realism: These elites say and maybe even believe that there is no climate change, but all their actions show that they know climate change is real. And indeed, during the past decades, deregulation, wealth accumulation, and overproduction exploded, with conspicuous disregard for the rest of the population, for life, suffering, and the future of the earth. The richest people seem to have made a clear choice to respond to climate change: Use their wealth to find a Planet B or settle in the few habitable places left on earth.

But Latour's realist rhetoric develops as a step further in the framework of this anti-denial argument: Understandably, Latour is tempted to counter this denial by emphasizing its inability to modify processes that are now irreversible. Hence Latour's reference to Gaia's vengeance, his prophetic tone, and his praise for a science capable of establishing factual truths. We must learn to despair, "we're locked in here [within Gaia] for good, double-bolted" (Latour 2017:81). "All that's left for us today is to recognize that we haven't prepared ourselves enough for the civilization to come" (Latour 2012:483). But is there a civilization that, come what may and whatever we do, is advancing in the shadows and will impose itself, in the same way that Atchafalaya "will end up capturing the entire river"? This assertion is incompatible with the definition of a plastic world governed by the agency of all its components. Contingency is the ultimate essence of such a "reality," one that consequently does not lend itself to the second-instance realism put forward by Latour: There is no fatality of Gaia's agency.

At the very most, we can admit to a third- or last-instance realism: To wit, one will not find anything more real than this open, plastic system, which is by no means a completed reality. The term realism then appears as misleading.

No doubt it is tempting to take the realist path and affirm that hypergrowth is *impossible* today, as it is coming up against the reality of the limits of this earth. Latour then reproduces the dialogue of the deaf between individuals stuck on different planets and calling each other delusional and ideologues, precisely because these isolated planets are defined not by suggestions and hypotheses, but by their exclusive concepts of true reality. To switch to a realist rhetoric is also to close the door to other *possibilities* of action and, conversely, affirming that an indefinite number of options are still open today also means accepting that hypergrowth is a possible choice that will perhaps define the reality of tomorrow.

In summary, the debate between realism and imaginarism is destructive and Coetzee's and Latour's most remarkable efforts to overcome it yield insufficient results creating confusion and inefficacy. It is imperative to revisit the concepts of reality and imagination. To this end, I turn to Shakespeare's *Tempest* for two reasons, which will be further explained in the following section: (1) *The Tempest* reveals the genesis of these now-entrenched concepts of imagination and reality, but also exposes their fault lines and opens up promising alternative pathways for today. This dual function is rooted in the premodern, early modern context of the play and the syncretism in Shakespeare's work, which make *The Tempest* one of the most extraordinary windows into the complex genealogy of the modern concepts of imagination and reality. Analyzing *The Tempest* within this framework will thus help us understand the powers of the imagination and its forgotten secrets. (2) *The Tempest* is also a key text in contemporary critical, political, and environmental philosophy, particularly through the works of Federici and Starhawk and, as I will discuss in Section 7, the revival of reference to witches and magic in contemporary environmental activism. From this political and ecological perspective, the central issue at stake in *The Tempest* is the confrontation between two models: The imperialist figure of Prospero and the premodern knowledge rooted in nature represented by Caliban and the witch Sycorax. I want to show that, in this political reading, which sees *The Tempest* as a crucial, yet overlooked, testimony to the early stages of the Anthropocene, the play suggests that the fate of both human and animal imagination was crucial to the rise of an ecocidal civilization and must therefore return to center stage in efforts to address the current crisis.

5 What Went Wrong with Human Imagination: Lessons from Shakespeare's *Tempest*

The Tempest tells the story of Prospero, a great sage and magician. Prospero, once Duke of Milan, devoted himself entirely to the study of the liberal arts, "neglecting worldly ends" (Shakespeare 2000:1.2.109). He entrusted his brother with the governance of his duchy, only to be betrayed and cast into exile. Prospero and his daughter Miranda are set adrift at sea and eventually wash ashore on a mysterious island. Prospero becomes the island's master, using his wisdom to command the elements and control the spirits Ariel and Caliban. Ariel, a spirit of the air, symbolizes imagination and intellect, while Caliban embodies bestiality and the untamed nature of the island. Caliban's very name evokes the image of savages and cannibals, reflecting the fears and fantasies of Shakespeare's contemporaries at a time when explorers brought back reports of their conquests of distant lands. Caliban is the son of Sycorax, a powerful, long-dead sorceress whose presence haunts the play, serving as an uncanny evil twin to Prospero. When Prospero's former enemies sail near the island, he uses his powers to shipwreck them and orchestrate a series of trials and illusions. These carefully staged events are designed to lead all the characters to greater wisdom and a political resolution that reinstates Prospero as Duke. In the end, Prospero abjures his magic and asks the audience to free him so that he can return to his dukedom.

What makes this play pivotal in the context of this Element is its demonstration of the link between imagination and magic, a connection that was crucial in the premodern world and will help us construct a more precise definition of imagination. The play also reveals a tension between two competing forms of imagination and magic: Prospero's "wise magic" and Sycorax's "rough magic." This tension is rooted in the play's historical context, as Shakespeare taps into the concerns and dilemmas tearing society apart at this cultural turning point. Scholars have long commented on this:[6] *The Tempest* coincides with the era of witch hunts, the early phases of colonization, and what Marx described as "primitive accumulation" – the violent transformation of communal or collective property into private ownership. This transformation was instrumental in establishing a capitalist economy and facilitating the boundless exploitation of earthly resources, of living beings as well as their fundamental means of subsistence. The transition from feudalism to capitalism was then taking its first steps, and it is impossible not to see in Prospero the emerging figure of a hyperactive manager, an authoritarian colonizer, a tamer of the forces of nature in the service of his own power,[7] all essentially linked to a hegemonic imagination, which I will analyze further in this section.

Sycorax and Caliban, on the other hand, embody a form of magic and imagination that is annihilated by the emerging new world. Yet, more importantly, *The Tempest* also shows that this magic and this imagination are not easily eradicated and that they are in fact still alive, in a hidden form, in the figure of Prospero and therefore in the modern world. Thus, pathways toward a different approach to an ecological imagination are not lost. In *The Tempest*, Shakespeare plays richly with the many facets of the various figures involved and does not shy away from the tensions and ambiguities that undermine them. *The Tempest* is therefore not simply ideological; the fault lines of what will become the dominant modern model, as well as an alternative model, shine through.

---

[6] For an overview of the critical readings of *The Tempest*, see Shakespeare (2000).

[7] "The wizard" as an archetype that haunts Western culture was brought to the forefront of environmental studies by Charles C. Mann in *The Wizard and the Prophet* (2018). Prospero was followed by a host of modern wizards – scientists, inventors, and technophiles – similarly characterized by self-righteousness and the power to control nature and achieve wonderful outcomes.

5.1 Imagination and Magic in *The Tempest*

In *A Midsummer Night's Dream*, Theseus defines imagination as that which gives to airy nothing a local habitation and a name, which is not meant as praise (Shakespeare 1979:1.1.16–17). Hypolitus immediately corrects this statement: Yet, through the story and the transfiguration of minds, "something of great constancy" (1.1.26) emerged. In other words, the artist, like the magician, manages to manipulate appearances with such power that the result cannot be reduced to a pure representation: It is reality itself that is modified. *The Tempest* takes a step further: Through the character of Prospero, imagination is defined as the ability to give *reality* to airy nothingness – for, as Prospero famously unveils, what we normally call reality is in fact *made of the stuff of dreams* (Shakespeare 2000:4.1.156–7).

To grasp the idea of imagination as magical – namely as an art of transforming reality through occult means that cannot be rationalized – it is essential to explore the connection between Shakespeare's ideas and the premodern conception of imagination, as well as the Neoplatonic philosophies that significantly influenced his work.

In many premodern texts, imagination is defined as the strange power to transform thoughts and feelings into bodies. An often-cited example is that of the pregnant woman whose fears and desires supposedly shape the fetus (O'Brien 1993:8). Imagination is therefore directly linked to magic: The witch can kill someone just by thinking about it. Montaigne also sees the power of camouflage in living beings as a form of imagination: "the hares and partridges that the snow turns white upon the mountains" (Montaigne 2006:147) are animated by a strange sympathy with the environment, a magical action at a distance that allows them to blend in with the dominant color of the environment, thus deceiving possible predators, whose perspective therefore becomes an integral part of these animals' plastic body. We will return later to this magical power from a biosemiotical perspective in Section 6.

These links of influence at a distance are also central in Neoplatonic philosophy. From a platonic perspective there is nothing shocking in saying that *we are such stuff as dreams are made on*. Prospero, a virtuoso at manipulating appearances, completely blurs his human companions' ability to distinguish reality from dreams and hallucinations. In fact, the possibility that we may be imagining what we think we perceive is integral to the human experience and a key to Platonism. It arises from the multifaceted and ever-changing nature of sensible beings: We can never be sure that phenomena manifest the actual presence of a thing because, despite some regularity in experience, gaps, and surprises persist in how things appear and reappear. Our world is therefore such stuff dreams are made of: the evanescent matter of Heraclitean appearances.

Admittedly, our world is not a mere chaos of appearances. Bundles of appearances crystallize, revealing a regular structure and recognizable objects whose properties are relatively consistent. Through myriads of changing appearances, regular features emerge suggesting general, stable ideas that we can conceive – for instance, the idea of the sea in general through a succession of many different faces. These essences effectively structure articulate and communicable human thought. Plato affirms their eternal and immaterial existence outside our world, and, even if one disagrees with this metaphysical assertion, it is still arguable that essences represent a dimension of surplus, existing in excess of the realm of the sensible.

The link between the Platonic approach and magic lies in the fundamental tension between a mysterious realm of ideas and a sensitive world in which the former manifests only confusedly and elusively. The instability and plasticity of the sensible world allows all kinds of illusions or surprising influences, as when the external appearance of the environment and the vision of possible predators are integrated into the external appearance of an animal: Snow is an essence that can *also* incarnate in the feathers of partridges. Discovering ideas through changing sensible bodies is a daunting challenge, but using these ideas to orient oneself in the sensible world is an even greater challenge. The realm of appearances and its love-hate relation with the realm of ideas – which makes sensible things sometimes instructive, sometimes misleading – intrinsically defies the human intellect.

Accordingly, *The Tempest* demonstrates that Prospero's neglect of worldly duties compels him to embark on a transformative journey of trials and exile, which teaches him to attend to his fellow humans and political affairs more properly. His bookish wisdom is not sufficient. His brother's betrayal and his expulsion from the city are the constraints with which his desire for spiritual independence collides. Wisdom is achieved by *returning to the cave* and grappling with the tension between eternal knowledge and the rifts, conflicts, and pretenses of the sensible world, which present an ever-new challenge to ideals. Wisdom is not separate from the manipulation of appearances, earthly powers, and political wins. Hence Prospero is a magician more than a mere intellectual.

The link between Plato's philosophy and magic is a central topic to Neoplatonism.

Neoplatonists argued that all beings in our world are secretly bound together by a universal sympathy, the most obvious manifestation of which is love and sexual attraction (Plotinus 1952:IV.4.40.5–26), but which also operates in like and dislike, alchemy and chemistry between bodies. The Neoplatonists value imagination as the ability to transcend the ossified realm of perception, shake off the boundaries between things, and make a way into other bodies and places through perspective-changing and empathy. They also claimed that there are two sorts of magic: An infinitely powerful magic rooted in the contemplation of ideas ("theurgy") and magic as a limited empirical art ("goety") (Curry 1959:177–80, 186). This distinction helps understand the contrast between Prospero and Sycorax.

The imagery of magic and demons portrayed in *The Tempest* comes notably from Neoplatonic philosophies (Curry 1959). But, as Barbara Mowat (1981) shows, Shakespeare mixes different figures of magicians, from the highly intellectual Neoplatonic magus to the street magicians, to create Prospero. Shakespeare thus shows the tensions at stake in his society, where magic as well as imagination is still central, but also contested. In early modernity, magic is commonly conceived as a form of tinkering and a set of risky practices (Tribble 2022); it stands close to the empirical knowledge of cunning folk. Spirits and the forces of nature are capricious; the sorcerer conjures them with fear and uncertainty. This stands in stark contrast to Prospero's nonchalant entitlement in his relations with Ariel and Caliban. A certain mockery of popular superstitions also begins to emerge, as the age of reason approaches. In this context, I will argue that *The Tempest* heralds a definition of imagination and reality, encapsulated in the figure of Prospero, which has come to predominate throughout the modern age and still influences us today.

5.2 Toxic Prosperian Imagination

It is no exaggeration to state that Shakespeare has become one of the epitomes of imagination in Western culture. In the works of Shakespeare, all is imagination. His plays are particularly whimsical and multifarious inventions of other worlds, illustrating the imagination's protean capacities for free transposition and infinite sympathy (Bate 1989:14–15). In this respect, *The Tempest* is a momentous play as it places the question of the power of imagination and its effects on reality at its center. What is more, Prospero is both the image of Shakespeare – the artist who stages and conjures the show – and the embodiment of creative imagination often cited by prominent philosophers specializing in the imagination as their reference figure.[8]

Clearly, Prospero incarnates the claim to a superior magic, founded in the intellect, a good magic contrasting with Sycorax, the "foul witch." Prospero is

---

[8] See for instance Sallis (2012:2–7, 97–101, 143–5) and the presentation of the Prospero Research Center on imagination in Brussels: www.centreprospero.be/.

reminiscent of figures such as Ficino or Agrippa (Mowat 1981), who combined philosophy with magic and made theoretical contemplation the royal road to transcending worldly confusion and coming closer to the gods. Prospero, the great magus, has achieved unparalleled excellence in theoretical knowledge, culminating in a god-like ability to perfectly understand and serenely manipulate the world around him. *The Tempest* shows that Prospero's imagination transcends the sensible world: He is the master who, behind the scenes, stages the dreams and is no dupe of his own tricks. It is precisely this Prosperian model of great shifts in worldviews that we see at work in environmental imaginarism described earlier.

The definition of imagination as an alienating force is present in *The Tempest* and Prospero's artifacts are ultimately meant to "comfort" "an unsettled fancy" (Shakespeare 2000:5.1.68). Yet Prospero embodies the force of imagination specifically used to fully integrate and concentrate all imaginative powers into the hands of the sovereign individual subject. With Prospero appears what may be the most personalized and subject-centered definition of the imagination ever presented. Shakespeare creates a remarkable hybrid here, integrating the premodern imagination as a magical force, imagination as a dangerous deceiver, and the modern imagination as a personal faculty.

While many early modern philosophers harshly criticize imagination as a nefarious and dangerous faculty, the enemy within,[9] Shakespeare finds a way to turn what could then be considered lead into gold, at least what moderns consider golden: *Individual personal* imagination as the key to mastery. Indeed, *The Tempest* is also a reflection on *and an intervention in* the process of the most systematic disciplining, chastisement, and subjugation of populations in Europe by the ruling class (Brown 1985:48). Shakespeare's strategy in this context is integrative: *The Tempest* realigns the imagination – which could then be seen as a rebellious force – by giving it value in the new system.

Therefore, the ultimate message of the play is: rest assured, "be cheerful" (Shakespeare 2000:5.1.302), "be collected" (1.2.14), and, allow me to paraphrase: "This story is unsettling at times; ultimately, however, it is not tragic but, at least to a large extent, comforting: Prospero – the imagination – is in charge and can be trusted, so all is well and virtuous in the end: please applaud!"

Of course, Prospero's figure is teeming with nuance and ambiguity, but the archetype Shakespeare bequeathed to us is that of a sovereign, personalized, gnostic, elitist, and hermetic imagination. Prospero is a stern and mostly coldhearted and self-controlled man. He embodies a strong-willed master as

---

[9] See for instance Bacon (McCreary 1973) and Pascal (1958:24–8).

opposed to a diffuse network of limited powers, a genius who remains solitary among his fellow humans (Corfield 1985:45). He submits everything to what he calls "*my* project" (Shakespeare 2000:5.1.1) – a project that he carries through from A to Z with clockwork precision – and summons spirits as his "*servants*" to, in his words, "enact *my* present fancies" (4.1.135).

In the same way, Prospero prefigures modern natural sciences (Spiller 2009), which fulfill the Neoplatonic dream and consecrate imagination while concealing its magical dimension, as everything is allegedly made explicable through mastered knowledge. As Kant (1998:108) famously points out in *Critique of Pure Reason,* it is only by vigorously compelling nature to answer our questions – by inventing and conducting experiments through artificially crafted protocols and the use of increasingly sophisticated technologies, rather than simply observing the spectacle of nature, as a more Aristotelian approach recommends – that we *force* nature to reveal its secret structures and the constant laws that govern it. In this approach the scientist is the master and nature the confused witness, not the other way around. In modern science, echoing Platonic philosophy, the scientist becomes the inventor, the theorist, the visionary, and the bold, independent, imaginative experimenter. Artificial and divisive fantasies pierce through confused perceptual appearances. And, indeed, many commentators have emphasized the parallels between Prospero and Bacon, another key figure of the epoch (e.g. Spiller 2009; Giglioni 2010). Prospero aims to enlighten his companions, even his enemies, and it is precisely through the creation of unprecedented circumstances – the vivid transformations of adventures staged by his imagination – that he teaches them to break free from their enslavement to the passivity of the senses.

In the art of Shakespeare and Prospero, sifting, parsing out, and reassembling – key activities in imaginative processes – play a decisive role. The island thus serves as a literary device that separates the real world from a world ruled by Prospero's ideas. On the island, Caliban and Ariel strikingly embody the conceptual distinction between wild, earthly nature and the immateriality and vivacity of the spirit, which are normally interwoven in humans. Here again, imagination separates and clarifies what everyday experience mingles. The swift movements of the imagination sift through the confounding rags of sensory experience to reveal the fundamental structure of reality. The storm is a second sifting device through which Prospero creates three groups of companions that ideally serve the scenario he has in mind. The illusory storm also embodies imagination's power to separate appearance from substance: It is a spectacle that causes no real harm. Prospero rewrites the script of his own life to transform and elevate souls, just as Shakespeare tries us by cutting us off from our familiar perceptual bearings and crafting a spectacle that challenges the imagination.

But Prospero is more ambiguous than just the prefiguration of the Modern scientist. Everything in the play constructs Prospero's distant authority by staging secrecy, referring, for instance, to his mysterious Art and Book, and contrasting him with the figure of Sycorax. The awful and cruel witch, who is conveniently absent and portrayed through slander and cliché, serves as a boogeyman, making Prospero appear as a good magician. We are not told what Prospero's wisdom entails or the nature of his magic. The play also suggests that Prospero's claim to virtue is, perhaps, the cover for a ruthless political intelligence (Kastan 2000:285–6). The audience may indeed realize, when the dust has settled, that, plain and simple, Prospero forces his brother to renounce the dukedom he usurped and, through a cynically arranged marriage, ensures that Naples will no longer pose a threat to his power. However, it is precisely because Prospero is surrounded by the aura of his supposed wisdom and white magic, that he manipulates everyone, including the audience. Here Prospero is indeed pure imagination as the faculty of smoke and mirrors. With Prospero, a fragile, yet mesmerizing and coherent, edifice is erected, an illusion akin to the king's divine body.[10] Prospero's and Shakespeare's manipulative imagination is used to impress and subjugate.

5.3 Sycorax: The Haunting Presence of the Witch

There are four sources of information for defining Sycorax: Her haunting absence, the testimonies of Ariel and Caliban, scholarship on the witch craze and early modern magic, and the figure of Prospero himself.

What we learn from Caliban and Ariel is that Sycorax was a powerful witch banished from Argier. She practiced an "earthy and abhorred" magic (Shakespeare 2000:1.2.326). Caliban, the son she "littered" (1.2.335), is described with demeaning animal traits and Trincullo calls him "a strange fish" (2.2.28). Without ambiguity, Sycorax's magic is tied to the more primal, physical, and dark aspects of the earth.

Contemporary critical literature has extensively underlined the haunting absence of Sycorax in *The Tempest*. Not only is Sycorax never physically present, but her character is portrayed in extremely coarse strokes through questionable testimonies. Ariel has met her but is oblivious to these events. Prospero, who arrived on the island after Sycorax's death, claims to substitute his own account for Ariel's memory, describing Sycorax with the most vilifying words and a seemingly disproportionate hatred. As for Sycorax's son, Caliban,

---

[10] See Kantorowicz (1957), the king has two bodies: a natural, mortal body and a divine, symbolic body upheld by political propaganda.

the few mentions he makes of his mother are certainly revealing, but Caliban himself appears throughout the play as possibly being a caricatured fantasy born of Prospero's dream of domination (James 1967:148–9).

It is impossible not to see in the absence and demonization of the witch in *The Tempest* a trace and reenactment of the witch hunts that were in full swing at the time. These persecutions represented extreme, systematic violence, coupled with radical dehumanization, designed to reduce a once vital aspect of society – threatening to early capitalist development – into harmless folklore. By terrifying the population and crushing revolutionary spirit, the witch hunts acted to suppress widespread resistance against the privatization of common lands, which was leading to migration to urban areas and the formation of a wage-dependent labor force.

As Federici (2004:205) has shown, the stakes of the witch purge went far beyond the simple persecution and extermination of women who practiced witchcraft. Indeed, after the witch-hunting period, individuals, including women, continued practicing witchcraft without being bothered. According to Federici, all women were targeted, and the witch hunts represent a major symbolic act that profoundly shaped modern civilization. First, the witch purge resorted to a divisive tactic – pitting men against women in a rebellious population – whose effectiveness is unrivaled when trying to defeat a numerically superior enemy. Second, the witch craze capitalized on existing gender inequalities, exacerbating them with relative ease. Third, women, more than men, embodied resistance to a system maintained by a propertied few, as they have a greater reliance on communal resources due to the constraints of birth giving and motherhood (25–6, 71–4). After the witch hunts, the image of the fierce and nefarious witch was replaced by a long-lasting alternative myth of women as inherently feeble, discreet, and ingenuous (103). Sycorax is silenced, much like women were at the time, rendered barely discernible behind the layers of the rulers' hallucinatory imaginary that animates Prospero's spectacle.

Yet Sycorax's specter exerts an overwhelming presence. *The Tempest* provides insight into the modern propaganda that, under Shakespeare's pen, carries a hint of mischief by not entirely covering its tracks. Sycorax is thus a more powerful imaginative aspect of *the Tempest* than the somehow very real Prospero. Sycorax's presence/absence, as it manifests in traces, is significant: It reflects not only her political and social defeat, but also the alternative world and imagination she embodies, both incompatible with the emerging "brave new world" that would give rise to the Anthropocene.

The Tempest shows that Sycorax has not completely disappeared. Better still, she is not only essential to the understanding of Prospero, but I contend she is also Prospero behind the facade. Therefore, Sycorax embodies an alternative and fundamental imagination. This point is crucial to understanding why the figure of Sycorax is key to our present times.

Specifically, Prospero defines himself in a typically modern way by establishing Manichean binaries: He is good because Sycorax is evil; he asserts himself as a masculine power, as a spirit ruling over matter, as a conqueror of nature, and as the human taming the beasts and bestiality in men and even more so in women. Oriented toward the ideal, he is the only one who can save a confused and conflicting sensible world. However, the facade cracks on several occasions, and the opposites blend.

First, the elephant in the room: Both Prospero and Sycorax are magicians. Although Prospero views himself as an absolute master, his power is limited. Premodern magic, openly embodied by Sycorax and more subtly by Prospero, involves a risky engagement with the occult and the uncertain. Magicians were thus typically marked by exhaustion and irritability (Tribble 2022:237–8), traits increasingly evident in Prospero. His anger and hatred when describing Sycorax reveal a venomous emotion that casts doubt on his supposed inherent goodness. This irritation also surfaces when Caliban's plot threatens to derail his plans, as Ferdinand observes: "This is strange; / Your father's in some passion that works him strongly" (Shakespeare 2000:4.1.159–60). Moreover, Prospero himself acknowledges that the success of his project depends on favorable conditions and "an auspicious star" (1.2.217). Crucially, by the play's end, when Prospero renounces what he calls his "rough magic," we realize that what was presented to us as a marvelous strategy for elevating and educating souls was, in fact, a series of somewhat disreputable practices (Corfield 1985). Additionally, Shakespeare borrows lines from Ovid's *Medea* for Prospero's speech (Orgel 1984:10–1), hinting that beneath the veneer of a white magician lurks a black witch, another name for Sycorax.

5.4 Sycorax: A Forgotten Earthy Imagination

To define *the form of imagination* embodied by Sycorax, we must draw on the few clues Shakespeare provides and Federici's research on premodern witches' magical practices.

To begin with, Sycorax's magical powers are pertinent in the context of a world that is not fully determined. Just as Prospero's magic is defined against the backdrop of the ontological claim that "We are such stuff/ As dreams are made on," Sycorax's magic is also rooted in a dreamlike being. Indeed, Caliban, too, speaks of a fundamentally dreamlike nature in a passage that echoes Prospero's discourse on dreams as the stuff of the world:

> Be not afeard. The isle is full of noises,
> Sounds and sweet airs that give delight and hurt not.
> Sometimes a thousand twangling instruments

Will hum about mine ears, and sometimes voices
That, if I then had waked after long sleep,
Will make me sleep again; and then, in dreaming,
The clouds methought would open, and show riches
Ready to drop upon me, that when I waked
I cried to dream again. (3.2.148–56)

It is notable here, however, that the impulse and the inspiration to imagine are coming from the island, in a less metaphysical, more embedded form than in Prospero's speeches.

We will look in detail at the link between imagination and a plurality of animal voices in the next section, which is also crucial to understanding the link between witches, imagination, and animals.

But let us first outline the nature of Sycorax's magic and imagination as earthy and rooted in the environment.

Federici did much to demystify the concept of magic in conjunction with her political analysis of the witch hunt. Witches, Federici claims, were poor, often elderly peasant women. They were more opposed to enclosures than anyone else because their livelihoods depended on gathering food such as fruits and herbs from communal fields and forests, doing menial service work for others, making healing potions, and trading in predictions, spells, and counterspells. Cunning women were also often accused of witchcraft as their key local role impeded the hegemonic power of religious and state authorities. They possessed empirical medical knowledge, many of whose recipes still form the core of the modern pharmacopeia (Ehrenreich & English 1973) and the witch craze led to the masculinization and subservience of the medical profession under the authority of the state.

Additionally, a significant diversity of daily tasks – by contrast with a highly specialized form of work – performed in symbiosis with the natural environment facilitated a holistic approach. The latter is characterized by attentive and patient observation of natural phenomena, including their interconnections and frequencies – such as specific paths chosen by animals, omens, or a certain atmosphere, something in the air, that suggest the likelihood of significant events. For this reason, it is hardly surprising that witches are commonly depicted surrounded by animals. The figure of Sycorax vividly illustrates these associations, both through her name (derived from *corax*, meaning raven) and through the story of Caliban's conception. This certainly resonates with Caliban's description of the knowledge he thoughtlessly gave to Prospero: "[I] loved thee/And showed thee all the qualities o' th' isle, The fresh springs, brine pits, barren place and fertile" (Shakespeare

2000:1.2.404–5). Sycorax's legacy to Caliban is an "earthy" magic based on the knowledge of the island, and without this magic, the heavenly Prosperian imagination would be nothing.

Such knowledge is intrinsically imaginative. Indeed, in a dream-like nature, there is no *absolute* certainty about the way a specific action will be furthered or hindered by the environment as a whole. The next section of this Element will further explore how animal imagination engages with this dream-like nature.

Federici also emphasizes that witches and sorcerers embodied a form of imaginative craftsmanship in voicing dreams and hopes in a way that is incantatory, provocative, and prophesying. Unlike the emerging attempts to establish hegemonic power in the Anthropocene, premodern magic bets on the relative ability of a prophecy to initiate a self-fulfilling process by modifying perceptions and behaviors within a group. Here magic perfectly illustrates the premodern concept of imagination such as outlined by Montaigne in *The force of Imagination*: Imagination is more powerful than physical causes, *Fortis imaginatio generat casum* – a strong imagination creates the case (Lyons 2005:46–7). Thus, as Federici notes, "Since the late Roman Empire, magic had been held in suspicion by the ruling classes as part of the ideology of the slaves and an instrument of insubordination" (Federici 2004:209). In this context, it appears that the Prosperian imagination of the Anthropocene uses the same magic but conceals its occult nature to make it more effective, claiming that all the phantoms it creates – the myth of the evil witch and of the ordered nature for instance – are nothing but the real reality. In contrast, Sycorax's magic remains a form of imagination that explores possibilities through tentative and inventive efforts, with no certainty of success.

The logic of the witches' magic practices was indeed non-hegemonic. To be sure, it is intrinsically tempting to present oneself as a powerful, hermetic magician to subjugate the community, yet the trust of the community ensured witches a more sustainable existence. Moreover, this knowledge was shared and transmitted from woman to woman and from generation to generation. Federici cites instances of creolization processes surrounding these practices in Mexico, where significant exchanges occurred between poor women of European and African descent and indigenous women, to the extent that it "became impossible to distinguish in it what was Indian, Spanish or African" (Federici 2004:109–10, 192–4). In other words, these practices mirror the plurality of voices and noises on the island by remaining rooted in a communal and multiperspectival form of power.

The intrinsic scatteredness of this rough magic makes it elusive, fragile, and imaginative. *The Tempest* teaches us that Sycorax is essentially weak, for to crush one's opponents, one must become Prospero. Let us keep this in mind when so many struggles today, in a state of ecological emergency, seem to yield too little. *The Tempest* illustrates how early modernity shaped the model of a powerful, masterful, and world-making imagination. The previous sections reveal how this model still underlies the tension between contemporary environmental imaginarism and realism, so that attempts to develop a powerful Prosperian utopian imagination backfire, reinforcing the Anthropocene dream by sustaining the very model of imagination and reality that defines it. Yet Sycorax's defeat is coupled with a quiet victory: Prospero is nothing without her. Though his power eclipses hers, she remains a haunting presence – elusive, weaker, yet irrevocable – undermining the logic of competition between them. The challenge today is to recognize and practice an earthly imagination that established order was built to invisibilize and suppress.

To summarize, Sycorax is the figure that symbolizes an alternative imagination defined as the ability to awaken imaginative forces in nature. This form of imagination connects us with the imaginative power that is inherent in the environments, animal behaviors, and the elements.

6 Ecological Imagination: Animal Imagination

In this section, we explore further the nature of the "Sycorax" imagination, which predates humans and thus helps us move beyond anthropocentrism. We examine its connection to a non-deterministic approach to nature and the rich imagination present in the animal realm, which we can recognize within ourselves and cultivate by altering our relationship with other animals and the earth.

6.1 Imagination before Humans: The Odd Earth

It would not be possible for humans to imagine if things themselves could not be present in both forms: As perceptually present and as "as-if" present. The power of imagination must be ontologically anchored; as the French phenomenologist Maurice Merleau-Ponty put it, "In order for the imaginary to be able to displace the real, real and imaginary must not be antinomies" (Merleau-Ponty 2010:181).

The kinship between perceptual presence and imaginative quasi-presence arises from the gaps inherent in so-called reality. What we consider real – namely, what appears through full-fledged perception, where sensory data are cross-verified – consists of aspects revealed in a sequence of perceptual manifestations (profiles, varying appearances depending on perspective, light, and other changes through time). However, this process of corroboration is never fully conclusive and does not enable us to predict or recognize all future appearances of the same thing.

Rationalism and modern science have done their best to identify more real, stable, even eternal and absolute structures behind the phenomena. However, their success has been limited. The emergence of relativity theory, chaos theory, and quantum physics has shown that science must also account for the inherent randomness and unpredictability in both physical and biological phenomena.

As a result, the stochastic approach – from the Greek *stokhazesthai* "to guess, aim at, conjecture" – gains traction in contemporary physics: Probability theory and statistical modeling techniques are used to approximate predictions of the evolution of systems characterized by inherent randomness and uncertainty.

Let us be clear: The dimension of randomness does not mean the defeat of scientific predictions. Chaos theory develops methods for understanding and calculating when and how nature makes leaps. But probabilistic and modeling methods introduce an irreducible dimension of ambiguity into scientific prediction. The development of different tentative models for the same system, and the fact that a minuscule variation can have exponential consequences, mean that the world is now seen as a myriad of processes that coalesce to produce a surface effect of approximate stability that can be massively disrupted. Chaotic systems are thus defined by "attractors," relatively stable patterns toward which the dynamic system tends to gather. These emergent relatively stable lines of development outline a future state of stability that is *possibly in the making*. As such they possess the quasi-presence or phantom-like presence that characterizes imagined objects. Some attractors, called "strange attractors" (Celso et al. 1987), are visibly chaotic and, non-repeating. Attractors integrate slight changes, most of which are negligible, but some may bring a radical shift to a new system dominated by other (strange) attractors.

The statistical approach clearly strives to *channel* what may appear fanciful and erratic, rather than to *play* with the possibilities that emerge in these ambiguous phenomena, but such imaginative play is ontologically compatible with chaos theory, whereas uniformitarianism condemns it as no more than a delusional and arbitrary psychological phenomenon.

What makes human imagination possible is both the dimension of uncertainty and the formation of *relatively* stable and recognizable, but fragile, patterns. Since the human imagination cannot exist without a dimension of ambiguity and non-linearity in things themselves, and it requires these structures of "relative regularity/leaps," I propose to define imagination as a process that extends far beyond the human imagination. Correlatively the Earth appears as a being that does not support a concept of solid reality. At best, only the concept of third-instance reality, as previously defined, applies here, to wit: We will not find anything more "real" by embarking on a quest for reality. Let us refer to this ambiguous and open-ended earth as the "odd earth."

Now, to define imagination as a phenomenon originating from the Earth itself, an extra step is required: We must turn our attention to the imagination of animals – something Montaigne and the premodern world already had a keen sense of, and that contemporary science explores in new ways.

6.2 Nonhuman Animal Imagination

Claiming that the earth is ambiguous and oscillates between various *possible* lines of development intrinsically involves the introduction of the perspective of a thinking subject. Without a subject that holds together, differentiates, and compares that which happens in fact, what may have happened, and what may happen, patterns of probability and events that break the regularity of the normal reality, there is nothing but mere present facts. Imagination involves the engagement of discrepancies and possibilities *as such*.

However, "thinking subject" does not essentially mean "human subjects," no more than "engaging discrepancies as such" means "consciously examining the mental picture of these discrepancies." As Gregory Bateson (1972:190) noted, when a mother chimpanzee withholds her bite to call her young to order and instead gives them a nip, this behavior connects the action – the nip – with what it *could have been* or *might be* in the future. This is how the nip becomes a meaningful sign: "beware," the nip says, "this is almost a bite – not quite, a quasi-bite – but it could have been a bite or may become one, so pay attention." The nip thus becomes twofold through a typical imaginative move that introduces a sidestep and a margin of play into the actual and the present. We can observe numerous animal behaviors that present the same integration of the real and the virtual. Think of all playing behaviors, but also hesitation behaviors or cautious/probing approaches in which movements are withheld and an oscillation, a progressive adjustment takes place – like when a cat prepares herself to jump or cautiously approaches a bird that she does not want to hurt with her paw. Here it is precisely the ambiguity and uncertainty of the environment, and of the body and other living beings that are revealed and engaged in the same movement.

A possible obstacle to the study of animal imagination could be formulated following an approach made famous by Nagel (1974): How could we have any idea of what it is like to think and, possibly, imagine, while being a bat? Instilling a phenomenological-existentialist approach, in line with Scheler's (2008:251) and Merleau-Ponty's analyses (1960:156–7), I contend that the degree of consciousness involved in such engagements of the virtual is of secondary significance. Indeed, when we puff out our chest and raise our head as part of a social role that requires a posture of authority, we can do it consciously or unconsciously and yet the *meaning played out* by the body remains the same. The intentionality which engages and develops this meaning is the same. Very often, in this case, the conscious representation emerges after the fact and the conscious thought recognizes itself structurally in a thought which was first played out unconsciously. Consciousness comes in degrees and all our ideas and emotions also consist of a certain behavior of the body, a certain state of tension, series of motions, or micro-motions on top of metabolic and neural variations. Imagining is first and foremost a bodily engagement with the realm of meaning (Merleau-Ponty 2012:139–43).

This engagement with meaning is an essential feature of the animal realm and provides the basis for what I call animal imagination. In this regard we can learn the most from contemporary biosemiotics, which devotes itself entirely to the study of the production and interpretation of signs in living beings. Biosemiotics has made remarkable advances in the recognition of creativity and interpretation in the world of life, thus overcoming the old mechanistic models as exemplified in the concepts of blind animal instinct and survival of the fittest. For a more detailed analysis of the intersubjective relations and cooperation that characterize the emergence of life and its evolutions from a biosemiotic perspective, I refer the reader to Louise Westling's *Deep History, Climate Change, and the Evolution of Human Culture* (2022). Building on the works of Jesper Hoffmeyer, Lynn Margulis, and Denis Noble, Westling (2022:4) emphasizes that living beings are essentially defined by their "aboutness," namely "their dynamic orientation toward or away from, openness or rejection of, substances and situations and beings according to their own needs." This notion of "aboutness" is crucial for my concept of animal imagination. First, I will explore its link to subjectivity, then illustrate how it reflects a dual and open-ended structure central to imaginative experiences.

The link between animals and subjectivity was put forward in a revolutionary manner by Jakob von Uexküll (2010), who is one of the precursors of biosemiotics. Uexküll based his theory on the observation of the ability of animals to create "bubbles" that are their own worlds (43). Uexküll terms this world *Umwelt*, where *Um* (around) emphasizes that this world is their surrounding worlds but also the world of which they are the organizing principle: they surround themselves with a world they project. Animals indeed select what is relevant to them and dismiss what does not interest them: They do so through their perceptive organs, through attention, and through what Uexküll calls their effect-organs (49). Animals *focus*; that is, they make specific objects stand out in *their* world, depending on their needs and how they use these objects. Through perceptions and actions, they interpret objects around them *as* prey, shelter, foraging tools. The "as" is crucial here: It indicates that an interpretive layer is integrated into things in the surrounding world while these things could be interpreted in many other ways: a dimension of choice, meaning-making, ambiguity, and creation is at work here.

Uexküll (2010:119–26) concludes: Animals are subjects in that they are not purely passively determined by their environment and, instead, project and shape their own *Umwelt*. They are the subjects *of their own perspective, interpretations, and initiatives*. This act of projecting a world beyond the given and present is a defining feature of imagination. There is even a hallucinatory and "magical" dimension to these *Umwelten*: For example a dog superimposes the image of an extraordinary, irresistibly adorable being on the human who is his master. Uexküll also points out that only migratory birds perceive migration routes (122), and he cites cases of birds chasing imaginary flies (120). Similarly he proposes the hypothesis – fruitfully taken up in several contemporary empirical studies – that animals turn to the world with search-images [*Suchbilder*] (Bond 2007; Tinbergen 1960; Uexküll 2010:113), which are general schemas of what they seek and lead to tunnel vision and partial blindness. Humans can experience this phenomenon as well; for example, when searching for a glass jug of water on a cluttered table, we overlook that the water jar is under our nose but is in fact an earthenware pitcher (Uexküll 2010:113).

If we can speak of animal imagination, it is also because *Umwelten* consist of ambiguous meaning through and through. In fact, entering the process of meaning-making essentially implies entering the realm of uncertainty. Living beings are embedded in an environment that transcends them, sustains them, and resists them. They are essentially defined by homeostasis and the formation of semipermeable barriers (Westling 2022:4) that allow organisms to regulate their internal environments while remaining responsive to external changes. Animals' ability to project their own *Umwelt* actively and creatively does not cut them off from constant risky interactions with the outside world. The structure inside/outside comes to existence precisely because of the semipermeable interfaces that constitute biological membranes. As a result, although the *Umwelt* is the external world shaped by the meanings projected by the animal, it always has a surplus that eludes the animal subject's understanding, hence its floating and imaginative nature. *Umwelten* are inseparable from the emergence of critical ambiguities, which can be grouped into two types of intrinsic discrepancy: The inner-outer discrepancy and the gaps between various worlds. Animal imagination is the experiential, behavioral, and symbolic engagement of ambiguities and possibilities as such.

First, the discrepancy between the relative vagueness of the searching-schemas and the resources available in the environment at a particular time creates room for all kinds of errors and adjustments. The life of animals is not without phenomena of misrecognition and misuse. Learning and attention variations also play a crucial role in the use of search images, and the ability to identify mistakes and adjust, through trial and error and/or an effort of attention, has been observed in a vast number of animal species (Blough 1992; Bond 1983, 2007; Clark & Dukas 2003). Even the ability to self-monitor mistakes and adjust accordingly was recently observed in rats (Kononowicz et al. 2022). The experience of making mistakes and the implementation of optimization processes in the shaping and responding to their world *implies the twofoldness that is specific to imagination*: It essentially consists in holding together present facts and possibilities, and in probing – virtually testing and comparing – different options. There is a fundamental kinship between this engagement of ambiguous meaning, which is structurally associated with the creation of *Umwelten*, and playful behaviors in that the subject must then hold together various possibilities as it ventures, compares, and fine-tunes different interpretations. *Umwelten* are therefore embeddedness with a hint of imaginative and perplexing distance.

The animal realm engages a second discrepancy: the tension between various worlds. Uexküll (2010:181) suggested that each species and, even possibly, individual is living in its bubble and that the various species complement each other thanks to the enigmatic intervention of a great composer. This idyllic image is not quite accurate. In fact, Margulis' discovery that the living world is symbiotic entails that life is integrative and dialogical. Symbiotic cooperation certainly involves streamlining, dependency, and mutual benefits, but there can occasionally be cheaters in populations of mutualists, and mutualism can turn parasitic (Frederickson 2017): This is by no means the majority case, but stable and successful mutualism, due to its intrinsic manifoldness, cannot be taken for granted. Thus, for instance, the history of symbionts remains dormant in the newly generated organisms, it can create instability, but can also constitute a "gene toolkit" with which the organism can "tinker" to develop new metabolic pathways and better adapt to new circumstances (Keeling & McCutcheon 2017; Ponce Toledo et al. 2019; Porter et al. 2019).

In fact, numerous ethological and biosemiotic studies show that interactions between animals bring their share of mistakes, image-creation – luring morphologies and behaviors (Dufourcq 2021:151–4) – fine-tuning and negotiations (Bekoff 1984; Ducouret et al. 2019), social learning (Shettleworth 1998:466–507; Whiten 2021) and creative attempts (Kaufman & Kaufman 2015). This is another reason to conceptualize animal relations to the world as imagination defined as a perplexed, dynamic, and creative intersubjectivity, namely interactions where subjects experience couplings and tensions between each other's perspectives. These tensions also require active and creative investment from subjects to harmonize with each other. Animal intersubjectivity involves exploring new forms of communication and cooperation that are not predetermined.

Timo Maran thus shows how interspecific communications includes the development of approximate and dream-like signs, whose meaning is not perfectly clear and determined, as they are simultaneously interpreted from the perspective of various subjects. "Ecological codes do not resemble human linguistic codes or algorithms but are rather like archetypal imagery or patterns" (Maran 2012:149–51). For instance dolphins adjust their vocalization when in contact with other species, and Herzing (2015) shows that synchronous and rhythmic vocalizations are also a tool that can be learned, fine-tuned, and implemented at various degrees in more or less successful attempts to create alliances with other rival groups. Symbols also emerge in this process – behaviors or traits that primarily function to represent or evoke something beyond their immediate presence, such as rearing as a display of power, nibbling as a warning, the play bow as an invitation to play, or the eye-like patterns on butterflies' wings as a form of mimicry (Dufourcq 2021:79–80, 143–6).

Animal intersubjectivity also gives rise to the emergence of transposition into the perspectives of other individuals. Ana Pérez-Manrique and Antoni Gomila (2018) offer a detailed overview of the current state of research and future development avenues concerning the phenomena of sympathetic concern and empathic perspective-taking in nonhuman animals. Further, in luring morphologies and behaviors, animals practically integrate the perspective of others into their world and adjust to what the others perceive, look for or fear (Dufourcq 2021:136–54; Maran 2017:124–8). When lures are implemented at the behavioral level, they can improve through the observation of the reaction of other animals. Both mimics or cryptic animals and their targets can enter learning processes (Cheney 2008; Gómez-Moreno 2019; Langmore et al. 2008). Here again we are presented with a manifold apprehension that attempts to gauge and integrate the conflicting perspectives of different stakeholders. The ability to transport oneself into someone else's world is a key feature of imagination. The multiplication of refinement and strategies in Machiavellian behaviors (Byrne & Whiten 1998; Driver et al. 1988) also attests to the complexity of these networks of relationships and shows that not remaining anchored in a single hallucinatory perspective opens the way to multiple opportunities to develop new tentative (symbolic) behaviors.

It is precisely this ability to generate morphological traits and behaviors, shaped and oriented by their intrinsic reference to what other animals perceive, fear, and desire, that Montaigne described as the force of imagination. Through *Umwelten*, imagination takes the fundamental form of generating meaningful, endogenetic, and malleable worlds. Subjective and intersubjective meanings become realities with the magical power to affect and mesmerize others – not merely through pre-wired cause-and-effect or stimulus-reaction mechanisms, but by incorporating active interpretation, learning, power relations, communication attempts, symbols, and negotiations. As a result, these interactions are irreducible to perfectly predictable or uniform responses.

To summarize, animal interactions with other worlds create buffer zones or transitional spaces in which the crystallized signs, interpretations, and habits are activated, leading to new processes of creative behavior, trial and error, interpretation, and negotiation. In this way, animal imagination is intrinsically embedded in – constrained and sustained by – an intersubjective imagination. Kant, German idealism, and Romanticism emphasized the link between nature's impersonal, transcendent imagination and the privileged human imagination. In contrast, I emphasize a plurality of embedded imaginations across human and nonhuman beings, where empathy – further explored in the forthcoming paragraphs – is key to interspecies communication.

Now, is what I have called animal imagination exclusively animal? Definitely not. Many features of nonhuman imagination such as described earlier also emerge in micro-organisms and plants. The qualifying term "animal" in "animal imagination" is not to be understood in a strictly categorizing, essentializing, and exclusive sense. It is primarily a question of emphasis and heuristic perspective. Indeed, in addition to the fact that humans are also animals, the animal kingdom is characterized by particularly conspicuous and pronounced disruptions in rhythm and differentiated phases of activity and passivity. The development of trial-and-error, learning, negotiating, symbolic, and playful behaviors in the animal kingdom at a pace and a scale that are relatively easily perceptible for humans makes nonhuman animal imagination particularly striking and lesson-filled for the human imagination, as evidenced by the overabundance of fantastic animal figures in the human popular and literary imaginary.

6.3 Lessons from Animal Imagination: Embeddedness and Empathy

Humans can learn two essentials from animal imagination:[11] embeddedness and empathy.

Animal imagination is glaring proof that creativity and distance can develop at the heart of practical interactions with the environment and other worlds. This

---

[11] "Animal imagination" refers to the imagination shared by human and nonhuman animals.

imagination is worthy of the name, but it develops distance, playfulness, and dream-like signs, *in conjunction with* processes of negotiation and tinkering to respond fruitfully to the challenge of pluriperspectivism and mutualism. Animal imagination is rooted in the observation of and the adjustment to one's environment, and thus *responds* to the imaginative processes that characterize the odd earth, while human imagination in the Anthropocene has become a tool to create bubbles disconnected from their environment. In this context, the human imagination can be seen as a specialized form of the animal imagination that has been overtrained in the dimension of distancing. This overtraining has led to an excessive focus on abstraction and detachment, which creates a built-in bias in our imaginations.

Human imagination indeed excels at creating the illusion of stand-alone abstract concepts and universal laws. Merleau-Ponty (1960:114) thus emphasizes that chimpanzees cannot easily repurpose a box they use as a "chair" into a building block; their thinking is embedded in the concrete situation. In contrast, humans develop symbolic systems that enable them to abstract ideas from their physical context, attach them to fixed words, and treat objects as interchangeable elements governed by universal principles. However, the stability of human symbolic systems is fragile, as concepts like reality, knowledge, nature, humans, and animals for instance are deeply intertwined with the fragile ossification of meanings through associations, habits, and social communities, influenced by significant power dynamics and negotiations among various groups seeking to shape definitions to reflect their interests and values. The illusion of stand-alone abstract ideas is precisely the source of the manipulation and self-righteousness that Prospero exemplifies in Shakespeare' *Tempest* and yet Shakespeare spilled the beans by insisting so much on the dimension of illusion, manipulation, and magic of the Prosperian wisdom. Retrieving the embeddedness and worldliness of animal imagination offers humans a way to develop their own imagination within a framework of truly horizontal attention to the environment and other *Umwelten*.

In this regard dialogical imaginative empathy is the second momentous lesson that we can learn from animal imagination. Empathy – from Greek *em-* "in" and *pathos* "feeling" – designates the capacity for and the action of perceiving the feelings, thoughts, and experience of another subject. Empathy is a controversial concept for there is no agreement as to whether it is possible to simply *perceive* the other's experiences. Although empathizing is not feeling-sharing (sympathizing), another's perspective cannot be reduced to an object. Transposition and decentering – a first-person grasp of foreign feelings – are necessary but challenging.

It is often underscored that empathy is based on reasoning by analogy, inference, imagination or speculation rather than being a straightforward perception of others' feelings (Apperly 2012; Dennett 1995; Lipps 1907:717–9). However, phenomenologists such as Husserl (1973), Scheler (2008) and, more recently, Zahavi (2014) have rightly stressed that, in our everyday experience of the world, this perception of others' experiences is primary and elementary (Jardine 2014). We are surrounded by beings with whom we interact in a way that integrates their perception of the world. Who doubts that this dog sees the ball I am throwing him or that this screaming, gesticulating man rushing at another feels anger? In fact, doubt is de jure permitted, but it is always secondary. Similarly, experimental protocols designed to determine whether a dog can perceive that we are unable to give him something, as opposed to situations where we *do not want* to give him something (Schünemann et al. 2021), can only be conceived in a world where we normally operate under the belief that the dog incorporates this information into his understanding. This belief is embedded in our intersubjective perceptual interaction with him and is not merely an assumption or judgment. From a phenomenological point of view, which begins by describing experiences as we live them before entering into more critical approaches, it is decisive to recognize the existence of this empathic perception. Moreover this recognition is crucial for fostering a more ecological form of imagination.

In the framework of a phenomenological approach to empathy, I argue that an accurate understanding of empathy requires incorporating insights from animal imagination. Only by doing so can we fully grasp the magical nature of empathy.

Indeed, the very tension between subjective perceptions and objective conditions – the inner-outer discrepancy – that is ultimately key to the challenge of empathy and makes empathy literally magical, is born with the semi-permeable membranes that define life. All living beings are grafted onto the environment, constantly exchanging with it, and are thus emergent structures of interiority. Therefore, like Scheler (2008:10), I define empathy as perception, but unlike him, I see it as an investigative perception reinforced by imagination, more than a simple grasping of a fully given.

Let me further substantiate this point. "Emergent" is an important qualification of the concept of subject, as it helps define individuals in a non-Nagelian way and understand how agency develops. An animal's interiority, its subjectivity, consists in an endogenic *Umwelt* that outlines a personal perspective, along with tendencies, tastes, and desires. This interiority acts as a virtual center, a point of convergence, a strange attractor, and an emergent agency. Where exactly does my self begin and end? No one can say, as my body prefigures my self, and I take up processes of self-maintaining habits and tendencies that began before I became consciously involved as their guiding force. This is what Merleau-Ponty (2012:139) calls the intentionality of the body. My body, like all living bodies, is autopoietic: It is a set of material parts that are structured in such a way that they become an active center which creates and maintains its own norms and preserves and develops itself following its own endogenous trajectories. My body recognizes its ways, skillfully manipulates things, already shapes an *Umwelt* through its sense organs and action organs, most of the time without my awareness. I *am* the gravitation of the whole world around this strange attractor of my emergent self, though it requires an extra step for me to actively embrace them and inject a new surge of agency into the autopoietic process. When doing so, I do not take up a process that is absolutely foreign to me, nor do I simply see myself in an absolute self-transparency in these anonymous bodily processes. My self emerges in between many anonymous bodily processes and interactions with the environment and others. A virtual elusive interiority emerges, yet not a clear-cut ego, locked-up within itself, perfectly self-aware and private to all the others, the kind of ego who would be the only one to *know* what it is like to *be* "me."

Now, in this context of horizontal attention to other animal bodies and *Umwelten*, empathy can be defined as the *dynamic engagement* of subjects with one another. Empathy is first anchored in living commonality. Our experiences and emotions, like those of other animals, arise from scattered behaviors, motions, postures, and interactions with the environment; they are not abstract ideas confined to our minds but rather a set of relationships and processes whose rhythms and styles can be taken up by other bodies – either through deliberate adoption, contamination, or a decentered "as if" attitude.

The science of animal welfare thus investigates how grimacing, contracting, fleeing from danger, and convulsing signify pain. Costello emphasizes, countering Nagel, that we can not only recognize these signs but also feel them in our own bodies as nausea and anxiety (Coetzee 2003). These experiences are both perceptual and imaginative: They are tentative and involve a quasi-experience of pain *as if* we were in another animal's skin. Empathy is neither a mere theoretical projection nor a simple perception of facts. It is a rich, yet lacunar, perception that initiates an imaginative process of dialogue and getting-acquainted.

Animal empathy pertains to magic as a risky leap outside of oneself and into an occult chaotic sphere. I cannot be sure that my virtual taking up of a certain open-ended style of being, of which I have a glimmer and into which I inevitably incorporate my own interpretations, fully captures what the other experiences. Animals adjust their empathic experience by checking with the other, asking questions, venturing gestures, and factoring in the way they respond. Through this interaction, the other also develops and discovers their experience. New structures and renewed selves emerge, as if 1+1 equals 3: A new dimension materializes from seemingly nowhere. Claiming to *know* what the other experiences is a form of hegemonic imagination to which we should substitute the negotiating and practical form of imagination that is developed in the animal realm in the form of dance-like adjustments to others (Smuts 2002:306). In these interactions, each partner observes the body language, signs, and potential intentions of others. This attentiveness allows them to adjust their own behaviors, whether by offering gestures of appeasement or displaying more provocative signals. For instance, an animal may initiate a friendly approach, gauging the other's response to determine whether to continue the interaction or modify its approach.

It is not surprising, then, that Vicki Hearne (1987:249) mobilizes an analysis of Shakespeare's *Tempest* in a book devoted to her experiences of communicating with various nonhuman animals: In training, she points out, we open up a transitional space that is a space of "rough magic," we take the risk of interfering with another animal's world and letting it interfere with our own. We take the risk of hurting them and of being hurt. But we also raise surprising possibilities, such as discovering a dog's sense of humor (61) or experiencing a horse ride as "a wonderfully rich and subtle conversation" (112).

The thoughtful image of attunement is sometimes used to characterize the embodied understanding that connects humans and nonhuman animals (Despret:125). This image highlights the dynamic nature of empathy, as well as the persistence of various individual musical lines that maintain their own autonomy. However, by defining empathy as imagination and magic, I aim to emphasize that empathy is not only inherently dynamic but also dialectical. It must embrace divergences and moments of cacophony. Indeed, empathy cannot exist without bold imaginative leaps into the unknown – proposals that the other has the power to respond to, reject, or distort. Empathy patiently awaits the other's response, ready for unexpected outcomes and embracing moments of dissonance.

7 Animal Imagination and Activism: Magic Now

This Element seeks not only to challenge and dismantle the concepts of reality and imagination that have consistently hindered our connection with the earth and our ability to effectively respond to the climate crisis, but also to foster a power that, by the conclusion of our analysis of *The Tempest*, proves both vulnerable and yet irrevocable. The animal imagination resists alignment with the new Prosperos – authoritarian figures claiming superior wisdom. Another key feature of Sycorax's magic is that it requires no prolonged initiation to access; it resides within all living beings, offering an immediate resolution to any Chandos-like dilemma concerning the supposed ineffability or inaccessibility of nature. While, crucially, this magic can be cultivated and advanced, its essence lies in what we, as animals, already think, feel, and do.

At the beginning of this Element, I outlined the tensions currently fracturing ecological activist movements. However, in the aftermath of Sainte-Soline, a wave of ideas and approaches has emerged that, in my view, anticipates the lessons of the animal imagination as defined earlier. In *On ne dissout pas un soulèvement* (2024 hereafter referred to as OS), a collected volume dedicated to supporting the activist organization *Les Soulèvements de la Terre* (hereafter referred to as *Les Soulèvements*), which faced dissolution by French government decree, Virginie Maris emphasizes the need to "thwart the military frontality that the phallocratic order seeks to impose on us" (OS60), arguing that this can only be achieved by overcoming the duality between ends and means. In other words, what we are looking for can exist now. In times of climate emergency, it finally appears that the utopian project to change the world completely, by undoing the all-pervading ideology and substituting another model, is overwhelming, disembodied, and, against its best interests, nihilistic. The radical utopian ambition remains, but it should be implemented in a deeply grounded form. As Maris puts it,

> experiences unfold that already foreshadow the desired worlds. We need joy right now. We need, without further delay, care, attention and solidarity for all those who for too long have been oppressed by anthropocentric, patriarchal and racist oppression. We need the rich earth of peat bogs and the living water of streams, the flight of the swifts and the run of the deer. We need this free and wild world that populates our dreams, our tales and our memories. (60)

In the remainder of this section, we will examine three central features of this movement that rely on animal imagination and help outline practices and representations that empower it.

7.1 Body-Territory and Animal Imagination

The focus on individual bodies, their needs, and idiosyncrasies is crucial to *Les soulèvements*. A chapter is thus dedicated to *care* in *On ne dissout pas un soulèvement*: Sophie Gosselin et David gé Bartoli explain that under the influence of the body-territory movement, *Les soulèvements* learned to systematically integrate a collective reflection on care in their processes. At stake is avoiding the reproduction of the Prosperian imagination's typical tendency to sacrifice individuals, their pleasures, and their sources of energy and regeneration to an idealized phantasmatic cause (OS:161).

The *cuerpo-territorio* theory, developed by Latin American feminist thinkers such as Julieta Paredes (2011), Lorena Cabnal (2010), and Verónica Gago (2019), underscores the link between the exploitation of women and the exploitation of land, echoing Federici's analysis of the witch hunt. It took shape in connection with activism against extractivism, in which indigenous women have played a leading role, and is deeply rooted in indigenous Indian cosmogony whose key is the fundamental solidarity between living bodies and the earth.[12] The concept of *cuerpo-territorio* reveals how extractivism is accompanied by a hypermasculinization of work and a process of derealization and devaluation of women's labor. This process of invisibilization, already evident at the rise of capitalism as discussed by Federici, is amplified in contemporary extractive projects. Women, often confined to the private sphere where men hold sovereign power, become invisible forces of reproduction. They are responsible for securing food and water in increasingly depleted territories, receiving neither recognition nor salary. Despite being the first to be directly affected by ecocides and to resist these injustices, they are frequently excluded from decision-making processes. Emphasizing the concept of *cuerpo-territorio* means refusing to allow a community to defend solely the earth when there are still women suffering on it (Cabnal 2015:80).

The body-territory approach represents a remarkable achievement of the animal imagination, inherently aligning with what Federici described as witchcraft. Indeed, it focuses primarily on the animal body, its fundamental needs, and well-being. The interweaving of body and territory manifests through affects, illness, desires, and sensations. A wound – though localized – can reshape one's entire relationship with the world, the *Umwelt*. As suggested earlier, the *Umwelt* is an imagination: It is not reducible to fixed perceptions but forms a dynamic, open-ended process of meaning-making – an imaginative mode of thought central to body-territory thinking (Sweet and Ortiz Escalante 2017). Hence also the growing significance of antispeciesism in connection to *cuerpo-territorio* movements and the identification of animal rights as a site of

---

[12] Indigenous philosophies vary greatly, with some incorporating forms of hierarchy or human exceptionalism. The connections between (some) indigenous philosophies and the mutualistic approach developed here through the concepts of animal imagination and witchcraft are beyond the scope of this Element and remain an avenue for future inquiry.

alliance to thwart the divisive strategies characteristic of the established power (Ponce-León 2024).

As a continuation of these ideas, Gosselin and Bartoli (OS:77–8) explain that, ironically, many activists have become worn out and disheartened by environmental struggles, only to be replaced by a newer, more energetic generation. This cycle reflects how the rhythms of the modern world have ingrained in us a neglect of bodily suffering and vital needs. *Les Soulèvements* stress the importance of recognizing those who provide food and care as essential to activism and warn against specialization, which fosters insidious hierarchies. "The concentration of knowledge resulting from the struggle often falls to those who are most available and best positioned to acquire it: cisgender, white, educated men in good health and without dependent children" (*Premières Secousses*, hereafter referred to as PS:75). Therefore, it is crucial for everyone to be aware of the physical, psychological, and subsistence costs associated with situations of oppression and with participation in activism. The everyday magic of witches, as described by Federici – and inherently intertwined with the multi-perspectival animal imagination – thus becomes a shared responsibility in environmental activism.

Accordingly, in *Premieres secousses* and *On ne dissout pas un soulèvement*, various members of the collective reflect on the difficulties and tensions I described in the introduction to this Element. Facing up to mistakes and challenges, along with raising a plurality of voices, combine to create a resolute mutualistic strategy and a clear commitment to embeddedness. "Ecology is not a new global condition requiring the sacred union of all earthlings to manage planetary catastrophe, as government transition programs and certain fringe thinkers [with a reference to Latour in an endnote] would have us believe. We are not fighting for the climate; we are fighting for our living conditions" (PS:67). At stake is to move beyond abstract appeals and recognize that our motivations and the energy fueling our actions are rooted in the soil that allows us to live and thrive. Ecological action should start from what sustains and heals our bodies, and the pleasures, pains, joys, and despairs of our daily lives. Embeddedness makes engagement more robust and sustainable. This is why *Les Soulèvements* focus on the struggle against the appropriation of land and water, specifically targeting the mega-basins and the sprawling cement industry that have been crucial in severing the intertwinement between body and territory in the Anthropocene. In this context, they stress the importance of understanding all entanglements in these appropriation processes to identify those directly affected and who could become highly committed allies in the struggle. Over the years, a detailed knowledge of the concrete sector and its ramifications enabled the identification of Achilles' heels as well as directly affected groups, such as village communities facing pollution or overexploited truck drivers (PS:38), both of which could become new allies.

7.2 Intersectionality, Mutualism, and Animal Empathy

The embeddedness of contemporary environmental activism goes hand in hand with the acceptance and promotion of diversity as a strategic weapon. *Les soulèvements* also develop through local committees and adopt a deliberately intersectional form, where feminist, anti-racist, and trans struggles, for example, but also exclusively symbolic as well as counter-violent modes of demonstration (PS:76), are intertwined, allowing a plurality of voices and modes of action to be expressed and solidarily coordinated without dissolving into each other.

This diversity offers several decisive advantages. First, this choice for diversity arises from the simple recognition – rather than an imperialistic and doomed denial – of a multiplicity of *Umwelten*, perspectives, and idiosyncrasies that is characteristic of the animal imagination. Moreover, embracing diversity is a way of creating a massive and widespread movement, and it allows for the emergence of a diffuse and polymorphous activist movement, which becomes extremely difficult to confront in one fell swoop or contain under the stigma of "a handful of allegedly terrorist individuals who should be locked up" (PS:61). Further, this context of symbiotic and mutualistic activism supports the claim that it is the Earth itself that rebels, as embodied by *Les Soulèvements*, and that it cannot be defeated. Indeed, although this movement is vulnerable, life as symbiogenesis remains the fundamental force without which nothing would endure, not even the Prosperian secessionist imagination and the modern ecocidal civilization. Intersectionality and animal empathy complement and support each other for three fundamental reasons.

(1) First, intersectionality was developed under the influence of feminists of color as an approach that recognizes their specific situation and subjectivity, which had been lost in the general process of rejecting categories as mere constructs (McCall 2005). By reintroducing the diversity of categories, not as essentializing concepts, but as tools to reengage the diversity of experiences, intersectionality relies on and promotes activism based on mutualism. From an environmental perspective, the concept of intersectionality is further justified by the Earth's multiperspectival nature. It becomes even more radical, as it then incorporates the need to address individual idiosyncrasies.

(2) Animal imagination reinforces the intersectional approach in another way. Indeed, intersectionality's raison d'être is also its permanent challenge: The relationships between different oppressed groups are inherently muddled,

forcing intersectionality into a continual battle against risky analogies and dubious metaphors (Socha 2013). This issue is particularly pronounced in efforts to connect animal rights with human rights. Marjorie Spiegel (1996) notably tackled the "dreaded comparison" between slavery and animal exploitation, accepting the associated risks and providing a meticulous analysis to substantiate the link. In contrast, Coetzee portrays Costello using the comparison between the Holocaust and industrial animal slaughter in the most heavy-handed manner, thus leaving her audience and the reader baffled (2003:73). Similarly, Adams (1990:66–7) strongly cautions against the use of metaphors in studying the connections between sexism and animal exploitation.

Here too, the difficulties encountered by environmental activism can be explained by the pitfalls of the human imagination and overcome through animal imagination. Indeed, the established order creates distant, wild, and contingent connections – between animal exploitation, sexism, racism, ecocide – by creating different dominated groups simultaneously. It does so by exploiting existing loose connections in the odd earth and popular imaginaries and by trying out different techniques of subjugation and exploitation in one group and transferring them to another (Spiegel 1996). The proliferation of these groups, the maintenance of their confused nature, their differences, and their rivalry are absolutely crucial to the established order according to the hard-wearing "divide and rule" principle. This divisive structure also creates opportunities for some of the groups to become oppressors and gain a semblance of superiority over categories considered inferior, which also helps the established order to hold. The sexual contract (Pateman 1988) takes this form, with the man becoming king in the private sphere. Likewise, in many societies, abhorred or heavily exploited animals structurally play the role of the ultimate scapegoat and outlet for frustration and humiliation.

Spiegel (1996:28) emphasizes structural intersections between humans and animals who share for instance "the ability to suffer from restricted freedom of movement, from the loss of social freedom and to experience pain at the loss of a loved one." If intersectionality manages to undo the rivalry trap, the mass and the Earth will rebel. But here lies precisely their vulnerability: The difference between these various oppressed groups and individuals is ultimately rooted in the diversity of perspectives and *Umwelten* that is intrinsic to the Earth. Not in the sense that these groups are substantial realities, but in that the imagination of living beings implies the creation and re-creation of barriers and blind spots. All may be reshaped, but the multiperspectival structure will not disappear.

That is why, as Kim Socha shows, intersectionality, as genuine intertwinement and solidarity, must be a subtle, case-by-case work of imagination within a concrete relationship with others accepted as such, an imagination fueled above all by what I have described as animal empathy. Socha gives the example of how PETA, a predominantly white organization, has used dreaded comparisons between animal suffering and genocide and slavery too often and too lightly (2013:229–32). She also explains how during a dialogue with a black student arguing that the meat industry is important to the economy, she insisted that animal exploitation is slavery: "if you eat meat you support slavery." The student was silenced and somehow vexed by the reasoning. The dialogue was broken. Socha concludes: "My activism is premised upon fostering compassionate perceptions of sentient beings, not shutting down dialogues with sensationalistic accusations" (2013:233). Words and abstract concepts can indeed become uprooted weapons of manipulation. Therefore, they should never be substituted for an embodied grasping of others' affects, their fears and joys, and their unique situation and heritage, namely for empathy as a skill that needs to be radically trained through interspecific imaginative interactions.

(3) Finally, it is crucial for intersectionality to integrate animal subjects both symbolically and literally. This path of development is suggested by Matthew Calarco (2020:21) and is expressed through different exciting contemporary projects. In a literal understanding of intersectionality as communality, *Les soulèvements* sketch up a world in which the communal spaces are regained on appropriated and concrete covered spaces and are seen as places shared by humans and nonhumans alike (OS: 121–4, 191). The concept of the commons as defined by Federici is crucial here: The commons essentially embody the interdependence between a community and a natural environment. The multivalent and open-ended purposes of living beings imply that the community hinges on the balance that arises from the free exercise of mutualism between species and activities, versus specialized overexploitation.

Therefore, also instrumental to this reinstitution of commons are the projects connected to the concept of *symbiopolis* and the reintroduction of animal species in living and working environments that have become excessively asepticized. Schmitz et al. (2023) thus present scientific evidence showing that "the restoration and conservation of wild animals and their ecosystem roles [is] a key component of natural climate solutions that can enhance the ability to prevent climate warming beyond 1.5°C." In the same vein, the *Manifesto for Abundant Futures* (Collard et al. 2015:328) underscores the need to integrate a deeper consideration of nonhuman animals' "familial, social, and ecological networks," including "their own lookouts, agendas, and needs," into contemporary rewilding efforts.

Responding to this call, Roggema, Rodriguez, and Tillie (2024) designed a comprehensive rewilding project that incorporates the concept of symbiogenesis. This approach to *symbiopolis*, within the framework of a rewilding project in Monterrey, includes the implementation of infrastructures alongside a monitoring team responsible for the continuous, adaptive re-evaluation and adjustment of these infrastructures in response to unexpected developments arising from interactions among various species within the rewilded environment.

An even stronger commitment to animal *imagination* in rewilding is found in the biosemiotic approach developed by Maran (2020). As living beings need to interact with an environment that they fill with meaning, the human-influenced environments should also be rewilded semiotically, namely, considered from the perspective of animal significations. An aesthetic approach is necessary to assess how shapes, colors, textures, and smells either disrupt the sign activities of other animals (e.g. bees interpreting road markings as flowers) or act as signs that can be constructively taken up within the *Umwelten* of the creatures we share these spaces with: Yellow or amber lights, for example, can serve as a compromise between the safety needs of humans and the needs of wildlife in urban nightlife (Longcore 2018). The challenge then lies in the diversity and discrepancies between *Umwelten* and interpretations of signs and the search for a holistic balance through empathy and constant adjustments.

7.3 Magic, Dream, and Ecological Activism

The last feature of contemporary environmental activism that I want to draw attention to in connection with what I have called animal imagination is its foregrounding of magic. The inspiration from poetry and art and the reference to the invention of new imaginaries, omnipresent in *Premières secousses* (e.g. 38, 53, 64) et O*n ne dissout pas* (e.g. 59, 70, 76 88, 110, 150–1, 157, 161–2, 166, 175), is not a new trait in the field of activism, but our previous analyses allow us to better understand how the myths and images of Gaia and the themes of daydream and magic – as they appear for instance quite blatantly in the quote from Maris earlier – can be used by environmental activism as an integral part of its power without getting trapped in the dichotomy between reality and pure fiction. This shows that mere empathy or mere intersectionality are not enough: The imaginative way of thinking and behaving is the key.

This theme is interestingly highlighted by *Les Soulèvements* in conjunction with the resolutely symbiotic character of contemporary ecological protests. The motto is clear: Activism must operate in the mode of tinkering. It is the cunning search for the right opportunity and the right allies without believing in the reliability of recipes which have been effective in the past. "We don't know what we are capable of until we have done it" (PS:68). Indeed embeddedness and mutualism do not guarantee perfect and certain success: Each attempt can fail and brings about results which are never definitively acquired or predictable. Therefore the polymorphy of living beings, the animal art of camouflage, and leaps of creativity are the model of choice and the fundamental communication tool that keeps the mutualistic cooperation fluid and open. Success depends on the formation of wholes that are more than the sum of their parts. New unexpected alliances have thus arisen amid the attentive and patient attendance of the concrete-cement manufacturing system and its hegemonic empire over the current world. Blue Monk thus argues that *Les Soulèvements* embody an activism that proceeds through leaps, surges of creativity, and, like jazz music, integrates phases of dissonances and divergences (OS:49).

Here the influence of Starhawk's work on witchcraft and ecological activism is particularly visible. It is explicitly put forward by Maris in her article (OS:59), and elsewhere by Isabelle Stengers (2002) who largely contributed to the dissemination of Starhawk's texts in contemporary environmental humanities. Starhawk proclaims herself a witch, a "priestess of the sacred Earth" (1982:16), and her model of activism is without doubt poetical and mutualistic (1988:300). In Starhawk's view, witches "[teem] with animal life" and (1982, 38) reconnect with the powers of the Goddess/ the Earth (1982:32) – which she explicitly refuses to define as a unified and transcendent entity (1982:31, 36, 38–9) – and they teach others to reconnect with them. Starhawk emphasizes the malleability of reality and enjoins us to "dream it into" a healthier, more pleasurable, and fairer world (1982:24, 27, 120–1).

I have reservations about Starhawk's often mystical definition and practice of magic. She frequently succumbs to an esoteric view of magic, a set of practices based on "visions" (1982:41, 45, 60, 102) that must precede action, along with daydreams and trances guided by an initiated person – a witch, priestess, or shaman. Her definition of magic as the power to change consciousness and reality at will (1982:80, 1988:40), adopted from British occultist Dion Fortune, unfortunately reintroduces the old concept of the individual, hegemonic subject. This aligns with the numerous spiritual exercises in Starhawk's books that aim to deepen consciousness and empower individuals. While emphasizing individual power is important in a mutualistic approach, magic is not a superpower; it is risky and only partially within our control. Additionally, Starhawk demonizes modernity (e.g. 34–35), often falling into the Gnostic pattern of radical conversion and rebirth (26), as well as the Chandossian cliché that words are inadequate to express nature's hidden power (57)

Starhawk, however, obstinately develops the antidote to these weaknesses: Recognizing that, as a witch and a priestess, she problematically puts herself in a superior position, she repeatedly and willingly exposes herself to the critical judgment of her companions of struggle (79). Recognition of her contribution should emphasize that she has brought back the heritage of New Age, neopagan practices, and poetical language experiments, to those who find in them tools for dreaming and tinkering their way into an earth-rooted existence. It would be a shame, however, if the key to earth magic, animal imagination, and contemporary activism were *reduced to* these practices, which were quickly imported into the world of team building and human resources (Stengers 2015:320). Yet Starhawk continually offers her readers the opportunity to experiment cautiously with the tools she provides or invent new ones, to connect sorcery with everyday mundane practices and simple communal activities (1982:16), and ultimately trust their own creativity and own boundaries in building communities. Her influence in bringing rich references to the original association between witchcraft, imagination, magic, animals, and equalitarian community in environmental activism is therefore without any doubt momentous.

8 Conclusion

This Element contains a diagnosis and a proposal for the reader's creative uptake.

Imagination is not primarily a human faculty. It is the engagement with the virtual, the absent, and the possible – an endogenous process of shaping oneself and one's world through meaning-making, creative ontogenesis, perceptions, and actions – found in all living beings. For humans, it manifests particularly strikingly in the animal kingdom, in animal morphologies, behaviors, and intersubjective relationships, which is why I introduced the concept of fundamental animal imagination.

Imagination is also enabled by the stochastic nature of the earth, which I have termed "the odd earth." This unpredictability makes every being ambiguous, unfinished, and only partially knowable; it lays the groundwork for a surface effect of perceptible and knowable "reality," undermined by indeterminacy, open-endedness, and space for possibilities and creative interpretation.

This beyond-human, earthly imagination contains the seed of self-intoxication, introducing an ontological gap between what is and what could be. It fosters the creation of world-bubbles (*Umwelten*), where living subjects may lose touch with other individuals and species. Though living beings remain porous and never fully separate from their environments and other *Umwelten*, a dialectic of imperfect dream-like communication, power relations, and manipulation of appearances is inherent in the animal world. Humans, especially in the Anthropocene, have taken the intoxication with imagination to extremes, which culminates today in correlative eco-denial and eco-anxiety, the recurring sense of disconnection from nature, powerlessness, and human groups inhabiting isolated worlds, unable to find common ground. While creativity and open-endedness drive life, human techniques, and scientific knowledge, they also risk fostering disconnection. The urge to project oneself into new worldviews, reshape reality through grand projects, and become "wizards" like Prospero in *The Tempest* also arises from earthly imagination. Human uniqueness lies in institutionalizing these bubbles through stable symbolic systems and ossified social structures.

Although human disconnection is never fully achieved, the Anthropocene cultivates a mesmerizing illusion of separation and disconnection: The belief that humans are no longer animals, that we have lost touch with nature, and must somehow regain contact with reality. It is also through this intoxication that the concept of reality develops, alongside its counterpart, the modern notion of imagination as purely psychological. This is no mere fantasy but a powerful construct that exacerbates ecological disengagement. Realism and imaginarism, as outlined in this Element, are both symptoms of this intoxication and the conceptual frameworks that sustain it.

In today's environmental crisis, this vicious cycle is in full force. Certainly, the ecological crisis challenges us to go beyond the narrow scope of the self and human-centric present, urging consideration of planetary scales. I do not mean to discard the relevance of this post-anthropocentric approach, but I have shown how attempts to formulate it have systematically brought about a realist or imaginarist rhetoric, inherited from the modern worldview they criticize, which has led to confusion and powerlessness.

The reference to reality and imagination is thus central to environmental debates today, yet based on shaky, unexamined foundations. I have challenged the modern concepts of imagination as a faculty of separation and unreality, and of reality as radically nonhuman, meaningless, and intrinsically difficult. Both the utopian stance calling for a radical break with the current system and the call for a return to raw, nonhuman reality conform to the same pattern, rooted in these modern concepts of reality and imagination.

I have argued that imagination, although it can create a narrative of separation, originates from an embedded form, where distance and creation occur within a network of intersubjective, meaningful – however ambiguous and open-ended – relations between living beings.

The analysis of Shakespeare's *Tempest* was central to this argument. It is widely agreed that this play is a thorn in the side of Western culture. *The Tempest* is full of lessons for us, as it embodies a form of thinking that both anticipates and predates modern thought, representing its embryonic stage, where tensions and still-unstable structures and concepts – such as reality and imagination – are at play. Two characters in the play, Prospero and Sycorax, continue to haunt our epoch, offering insights into the genesis of what I have called intoxication on imagination. From *The Tempest*, we learn that we are all both Prospero and Sycorax, and that imagination and reality are inseparable. Reality is shaped by the wizards who cultivate a separate imagination – or, more accurately, the illusion thereof – while remaining dependent on a more fundamental imagination expressed by Sycorax and Caliban, reflecting the voices and dreams of the Earth. I have shown how this poetic description aligns with and can be substantiated through a biosemiotic approach to living beings and their environment.

Ultimately, this Element proposes actively choosing vulnerability as a sustainable power and reconnecting with and empowering the animal imagination. This reconnection is not revolutionary in the modern sense; we have never fully lost this connection. Any narrative framing this reconnection with animality or the earth as "difficult" – in Diamond's sense of reality – and avant-garde reflects modernity's tired competition over who is most groundbreaking and closest to reality.

In contrast with both utopian and realist approaches, the animal imagination within us and in our interactions with other living beings grounds us in a present full of possibilities, interpretation, agency, empathy, and mutualistic imagination. This perspective allows us to envision the future from a present where imagination can actively engage with the environment.

This imagination is humble and inclusive in that, self-aware as imagination, it recognizes that it offers new models and images while remaining magical – namely daring and vulnerable. It cannot dictate or fully predict the responses of other beings and milieus, yet it actively imagines and realizes mutualistic networks. As such, ecological imagination *really* interacts with the world and other imaginations, fostering genuine intersectionality and resisting realignment by capitalistic logics of competition, authority, or superficial fantasies.

This embedded and empathetic animal imagination is central to what Federici describes as a forgotten witchcraft beyond romanticization and mysticism. I have shown that it is already prominent in various aspects of contemporary environmental activism and should be viewed as a reservoir of sustainable practices within our reach. We will not invent anything radically new (PS:20); yet it is our task to be bold and creative in dialogue with an earthly imagination.

References

Abram, D. 1991. "The Mechanical and the Organic: On the Impact of Metaphor in Science." In S. Schneider and P. Boston (eds.), *Scientists on Gaia*. Cambridge, MA: MIT Press, pp. 67–74.

———. 2011. *Becoming Animal: An Earthly Cosmology*. New York: Vintage books.

Adams, C. 1990. *The Sexual Politics of Meat*. New York: Bloomsbury Academic.

Apperly, I. A. 2012. "What Is 'Theory of Mind'? Concepts, Cognitive Processes and Individual Differences." *The Quarterly Journal of Experimental Psychology*, 65, no. 5, 825–39.

Attridge, D. 2004. "Ethical Modernism: Servants as Others in J. M. Coetzee's Early Fiction." *Poetics Today*, 25, no. 4, 653–71.

Bate, J. 1989. *Shakespeare and the English Romantic Imagination*. Oxford: Oxford University Press.

Bateson, G. 1972. *Steps to an Ecology of Mind*. Northvale, NJ: Jason Aronson.

Bekoff, M. 1984. "Social Play Behavior." *BioScience*, 34, no. 4, 228–33.

Blaut, J. M. 1993. *The Colonizer's Model of the World: Geographical Diffusionism and Eurocentric History*. New York: Routledge.

Blough, P. M. 1992. "Detectability and Choice during Visual Search: Joint Effects of Sequential Priming and Discriminability." *Animal Learning and Behaviour*, 20, 293–300.

Bond, A. B. 1983. "Visual Search and Selection of Natural Stimuli in the Pigeon: The Attention Threshold Hypothesis." *Journal of Experimental Psychology: Animal Learning and Cognition* 9, 292–306.

———. 2007. "The Evolution of Color Polymorphism: Crypticity, Searching Images, and Apostatic Selection." *Annual Review of Ecology, Evolution, and Systematics*, 38, 489–514.

Brown, P. 1985. "'This Thing of Darkness I Acknowledge Mine': The Tempest and the Discourse of Colonialism." In J. Dollimore and A. Sinfield (eds.), *Political Shakespeare: New Essays Cultural Materialism*. Ithaca, NY: Cornell University Press, pp. 48–71.

Buell, L. 1996. *The Environmental Imagination: Thoreau, Nature Writing, and the Formation of American Culture*. Cambridge, MA: The Belknap Press.

Byrne, R. W. and A. Whiten (Eds.). 1998. *Machiavellian Intelligence: Social Expertise and the Evolution of Intellect in Monkeys, Apes, and Humans*. Oxford: Clarendon Press.

Cabnal, L. 2010. "Acercamiento a la construcción de la propuesta de pensamiento epistémico de las mujeres indígenas feministas comunitarias de Abya Yala." In *Feminismos diversos: el feminismo comunitario*. Madrid: Acsur Las Segovias, pp. 10–25. Available at: https://porunavidavivible.files.wordpress.com/2012/09/feminismos-comunitario-lorena-cabnal.pdf. Accessed on: October 16, 2018.

    2015. "Corps-territoire et territoire-Terre: le féminisme communautaire au Guatemala." Interview by J. Falquet. *Cahiers du Genre*, 2015/2(59), 73–89. Éditions Association Féminin Masculin Recherches.

Calarco, M. 2020. *Beyond the Anthropological Difference*. Elements in Environmental Humanities. Cambridge: Cambridge University Press.

Celso, G., E. Ott, and J. A. Yorke. 1987. "Chaos, Strange Attractors, and Fractal Basin Boundaries in Nonlinear Dynamics." *Science*, 238, no. 4827, 632–8.

Chakrabarty, D. 2021. *The Climate of History in a Planetary Age*. Chicago, IL: The University of Chicago Press.

Cheney, K. L. 2008. "The Role of Avoidance Learning in an Aggressive Mimicry System." *Behavioral Ecology*, 19, no. 3, 583–8, https://doi.org/10.1093/beheco/arn001.

Clark, C. W. and R. Dukas. 2003. "The Behavioral Ecology of a Cognitive Constraint: Limited Attention." *Behavioral Ecology*, 14, no. 2 (March): 151–6. https://doi.org/10.1093/beheco/14.2.151.

Clark, T. 2015. *Ecocriticism on the Edge: The Anthropocene as a Threshold Concept*. London: Bloomsbury.

Coetzee, J. M. 2003. *Elizabeth Costello*. London: Viking.

Collard, R. C., J. Dempsey, and J. Sundberg. 2015. "A Manifesto for Abundant Futures." *Annals of the Association of American Geographers*, 105, no. 2, 322–30.

Corfield, C. 1985. "Why Does Prospero Abjure His 'Rough Magic'?" *Shakespeare Quarterly*, 36, no. 1 (Spring), 31–48.

Curry, W. C. 1959. *Shakespeare's Philosophical Patterns*. Baton Rouge: Louisiana State University Press.

Del Fa, S. 2023. "Comment les Soulèvements de la Terre fédèrent une nouvelle écologie radicale et sociale." In *The Conversation*, April 27.

Deleuze, G. 1994. *Difference and Repetition*. Eng. trans. P. Patton. New York: Columbia University Press.

Deleuze, G. and F. Guattari. 1988. *A Thousand Plateaus*. Trans. B. Massumi. London: Athlone.

Dennett, D. 1995. "Do Animals Have Beliefs?" In H. Roitblat (ed.), *Comparative Approaches to Cognitive Sciences*. London: MIT Press, pp. 111–8.

Despret, V. 2004. "The Body We Care For: Figures of Anthropo-Zoo-Genesis." *Body and Society.* Special Issue on "Bodies on Trial," 10, nos. 2–3, 111–34.

Diamond, C. 1991. *The Realistic Spirit.* Cambridge, MA: MIT Press.

2008. "The Difficulty of Reality and the Difficulty of Philosophy." In S. Cavell, C. Diamond, J. McDowell, I. Hacking, and C. Wolfe, *Philosophy and Animal Life.* New York: Columbia University Press, pp. 43–90.

Driver, P. M. and D. A. Humphries. 1988. *Protean Behaviour: The Biology of Unpredictability.* Oxford: Clarendon Press.

Ducourcq, P. A. Romano, A. N., Dreiss, P. et al. 2019. "The Art of Diplomacy in Vocally Negotiating Barn Owl Siblings." *Frontiers in Ecology and Evolution*, Vol. 7 (September) (Online).

Dufourcq, A. 2021. *The Imaginary of Animals.* New York: Routledge.

Ehrenreich, B. and D. English. 1973. *Witches, Midwives, & Nurses: A History of Women Healers.* Second Ed. Old Westbury, NY: The Feminist Press.

Extinction Rebellion. 2022. "We Quit." December 31, https://extinctionrebellion.uk/2022/12/31/we-quit/.

Federici, S. 2004. *Caliban and the Witch: Women, the Body, and Primitive Accumulation.* Brooklyn, NY: Autonomedia.

Ferraris, M. 2020. *Manifesto of New Realism.* Albany, NY: SUNY.

Frederickson, M. E. 2017. "Mutualisms Are Not on the Verge of Breakdown." *Trends in Ecology & Evolution*, 32, no. 546, 727–34.

Frisch, S. 2014. "How Cognitive Neuroscience Could Be More Biological – and What It Might Learn from Clinical Neuropsychology." In *Frontiers in Human Neuroscience*, Vol. 8, 541.

Gago, V. 2019. *La potencia feminista: o el deseo de cambiarlo todo.* Ciudad Autónoma de Buenos Aires: Tinta Limón.

Ghosh, A. 2016. *The Great Derangement: Climate Change and the Unthinkable.* Chicago: University of Chicago Press.

Giglioni, G. 2010. "Fantasy Islands: Utopia, the Tempest, and New Atlantis as Places of Controlled Credulousness." In A. B. Kavey (ed.), *World-Building and the Early Modern Imagination.* New York: Palgrave Macmillan, pp. 91–117.

Gómez-Moreno, J. M. U. 2019. "The 'Mimic' or 'Mimetic' Octopus? A Cognitive-Semiotic Study of Mimicry and Deception in Thaumoctopus Mimicus." *Biosemiotics*, 12 (December), 441–67.

Gould, S. J. 1987. *Time's Arrow, Time's Cycle: Myth and Metaphor in the Discovery of Geological Time.* Cambridge, MA: Harvard University Press.

Hearne, V. 1987. *Adam's Task: Calling Animals by Name.* New York: Knopf.

Herzing, L. D. 2015. "Synchronous and Rhythmic Vocalizations and Correlated Underwater Behavior of Free-Ranging Atlantic Spotted Dolphins (Stenella frontalis) and Bottlenose Dolphins (Tursiops truncatus) in the Bahamas." *Animal Behavior and Cognition*, 2, 14–29.

Hofmannsthal, H. von. 1979. *Der Dichter und diese Zeit*, Gesammelte Werke in zehn Einzelbänden, Band 8, Reden und Aufsätze I, Fischer, Frankfurt.

Hofmannsthal, H. von. 2008. "The Letter of Lord Chandos." In J. DonaldMcClatchy (ed.), *The Whole Difference: Selected Writings of Hugo von Hofmannsthal*. Trans. T. Stern and J. Stern. Princeton, NJ: Princeton University Press.

Hsu, H. 2020. "The Search for New Words to Make Us Care about the Climate Crisis." *The New Yorker*, February 21.

Husserl, E. 1973. *Zur Phänomenologie der Intersubjektivität. Texte aus dem Nachlaß, Zweiter Teil: 1921–1928*. The Hague: M. Nijoff.

James, D. G. 1967. *The Dream of Prospero*. Oxford: Oxford University Press.

Jardine, J. 2014. "Husserl and Stein on the Phenomenology of Empathy: Perception and Explication." *Synthesis Philosophica*, 29, no. 2, 273–88.

Kant, I. 1998. *Critique of Pure Reason*. Trans. P. Guyer and A. W. Wood. Cambridge: Cambridge University Press.

Kantorowicz, E. 1957. *The King's Two Bodies: A Study on Medieval Political Theology*. Princeton: Princeton University Press.

Kastan, D. S. 2000. "'The Duke of Milan / And His Brave Son': Old Histories and New in The Tempest." In W. Shakespeare, G. Graff, and J. Phelan (eds.), *The Tempest. A Case Study in Critical Controversy*. Boston, NY: Bedford/St. Martin's.

Kaufman, A. B. and J. C. Kaufman. 2015 (Eds). *Animal Creativity and Innovation*. London: Elsevier.

Keeling, P. and J. McCutcheon. 2017. "Endosymbiosis: The Feeling Is Not Mutual." *Journal of Theoretical Biology*, 7, no. 434 (December) 75–9.

Kirchner, J. W. 1990. "Gaia Metaphor Unfalsifiable." *Nature*, 345, no. 6275 (June) 470.

Klopper, D. 2008. "'We Are Not Made for Revelation': Letters to Francis Bacon in the Postscript to J. M. Coetzee's Elizabeth Costello." *English in Africa*; Grahamstown, 35, no. 2 (October) 119–32.

Kononowicz, T. W., V. van Wassenhove, and V. Doyère. 2022. "Rodents Monitor Their Error in Self-Generated Duration on a Single Trial Basis." *Proceedings of the National Academy of Sciences*, 119, no. 9, (online).

Langmore, N. E., G. Maurer, G. Adcock, and R. M. Kilner. 2008. "Socially Acquired Host-Specific Mimicry and the Evolution of Host Races in

Horsfield's Bronze-Cuckoo Chalcites Basalis." *Evolution*, 62, no. 7 (July). 1689–99.

Latour, B. 1993. *We Have Never Been Modern*. Cambridge, MA: Harvard University Press.

2009. *Sur le culte des dieux faitiches: Suivi de Iconoclash*. Paris: La Découverte.

2012. *Enquête sur les modes d'existence*. Paris: La Découverte.

2017. *Facing Gaia: Eight Lectures on the New Climatic Regime*. Cambridge: Polity Press.

2018. *Down to Earth: Politics in the New Climatic Regime*. Cambridge: Polity Press.

2019. "Extending the Domain of Freedom, or Why Is Gaia so Hard to Understand?" 45, no. 3: 659–680.

2020a. *The Parliament of Things*. Radboud University, November 23, 2020. Video. www.youtube.com/watch?v=zZF9gbQ7iCs&ab_channel=Radboud Reflects.

2020b. Bruno Latour, Entretien avec Andrew Todd, *The Guardian*, February 4, 2020.

Le Guin, U. K. 2007. "The Critics, the Monsters, and the Fantasists." *The Wordsworth Circle*, 38, no. 1/2, 83-7.

Les Soulèvements de la Terre. 2023. "A celles et ceux qui ont marché à Sainte-Soline." https://lessoulevementsdelaterre.org/blog/a-celles-et-ceux-qui-ont-marche-a-sainte-soline.

2024. *Premières secousses*. Paris: La Fabrique.

Lipps, T. 1907. "Das Wissen von fremden Ichen." In T. Lipps, *Psychologische Untersuchungen I*. Leipzig: Engelmann, 694–722.

Longcore, T. 2018 "Rapid Assessment of Lamp Spectrum to Quantify Ecological Effects of Light at Night." *The Journal of Experimental Zoology – A*, 329, nos. 8–9 (October), 694–722.

Lotman, J. and W. Clark. 2005. "On the Semiosphere." *Semiotica: Sign Systems Studies*, 13, no. 1, 205–26.

Lovelock, J. 1988. *The Ages of Gaia: A Biography of Our Living Earth*. New York: Norton.

Lyons, J. D. 2005. *Before Imagination: Embodied Thought from Montaigne to Rousseau*. Redwood: Stanford University Press.

Maran, T. 2012. "Are Ecological Codes Archetypal Structures?" In T. Maran, K. Lindström, R. Magnus, and M. Tønnessen (Eds.), *Semiotics in the Wild: Essays in Honour of Kalevi Kull on the Occasion of His 60th Birthday*. Tartu: University of Tartu Press, 147–56.

2017. *Mimicry and Meaning: Structure and Semiotics of Biological Mimicry*. Dordrecht: Springer.

2020. *Ecosemiotics: The Study of Signs in Changing Ecologies*. Cambridge: Cambridge University Press.

McCall, L. 2005. "The Complexity of Intersectionality." *Signs*, 30, no. 3 (Spring).

McCreary, E. P. 1973. "Bacon's Theory of Imagination Reconsidered." *The Huntington Library Quarterly*, 36, no. 4 (August), 317–26.

Meillassoux, Q. 2009. *After Finitude: An Essay on the Necessity of Contingency*. Trans. R. Brassier. New York: Continuum.

Merleau-Ponty, M. 1960. *The Structure of Behavior*. Trans. Alden Fisher. Boston, MA: Beacon Press.

2010. *Child Psychology and Pedagogy: The Sorbonne Lectures, 1949–1952*. Trans. T. Welsh. Evanston, IL: Northwestern University Press.

2012. *Phenomenology of Perception*. Trans. D. Landes. New York: Routledge.

Mitra, M. N. 2019 "Less Talk, More Action." *Earth Island Journal* 2029 (Winter), www.earthisland.org/journal/index.php/magazine/entry/less-talk-more-action/##.

Montaigne, M. de. 2006. "Of the Force of Imagination." Trans. Charles Cotton. 1574. *Quotidiana*. Ed. Patrick Madden. December 26, 2006. July 30, 2024.

Mowat, B. A. 1981. "Prospero, Agrippa, and Hocus Pocus." *English Literary Renaissance*, 11, no. 3 (Autumn), 281–303.

2001. "Prospero's Book." *Shakespeare Quarterly*, 52, no. 1 (Spring).

Naess, A. 1973. "The Shallow and the Deep, Long-Range Ecology Movement: A Summary." In A. Drengson and H. Glasser (eds.), *Selected Works of Arne Naess, X*. Dordrecht: Springer, pp. 7–12.

Nagel, T. 1974. "What Is It Like to Be a Bat?" *The Philosophical Review*, 83, no. 4, 435–50.

Nietzsche, F. 2020. "About Truth and Lie in the Extra-Moral Sense." In *Nietzsche's Seven Notebooks from 1876*. Trans. by D. F. Ferrer, Internet Archive.

Norris, M. 1985. *Beasts of the Modern Imagination: Darwin, Nietzsche, Kafka, Ernst, and Lawrence*. Baltimore: Johns Hopkins University Press.

O'Brien, J. 1993. "Reasoning with the Senses: The Humanist Imagination." *South Central Review*, 10, no. 2, 3–19.

On ne dissout pas un soulèvement. 40 voix pour les Soulèvements de la Terre. 2023. Paris: Seuil.

Onori, L. and G. Visconti. 2012. "The GAIA Theory: From Lovelock to Margulis. From a Homeostatic to a Cognitive Autopoietic Worldview." *Rendiconti Lincei*, June 26.

Orgel, S. 1984. "Prospero's Wife." *Representations*, no. 8 (Autumn), 1–13.

Paredes, J. 2011. *Hilando Fino, desde el feminismo comunitario*. La Paz: Comunidad Mujeres Creando Comunidad.

Parini, J. 1995. "The Greening of the Humanities." *The New York Times Magazine*, October 29.

Pateman, C. 1988. *The Sexual Contract*. Redwood City: Stanford University Press.

Pérez-Manrique, A. and A. Gomila. 2018. "The Comparative Study of Empathy: Sympathetic Concern and Empathic Perspective-Taking in Non-human Animals." *Biological Reviews*, 93, no. 1, 248–69.

Plotinus. 1952. *Enneads*. Translated by S. Mackenna and B. S. Page https://classics.mit.edu/Plotinus/enneads.html.

Plumwood, V. 1993. *Feminism and the Mastery of Nature*. New York: Routledge.

Ponce-León, J. J. 2024. "Feminismos antiespecistas en Ecuador y Colombia: prácticas queer y veganismos decoloniales." *Íconos. Revista de Ciencias Sociales*, 78, 177–97.

Ponce Toledo, R. I., P. Lopez-Garcia, and D. Moreira. 2019. "Horizontal and Endosymbiotic Gene Transfer in Early Plastid Evolution." *The New Phytologist*, 224, no. 2, 618–24.

Porter, S. S., J. Faber-Hammond, A. P. Montoya, M. L. Friesen, and C. Sackos. 2019. "Dynamic Genomic Architecture of Mutualistic Cooperation in a Wild Population of Mesorhizobium." *The ISME Journal*, 13, no. 2, 301–15.

Roggema, R., Rodriguez, D., and Tillie, N. 2024. "When the Bear Comes to Town: How the City Could Create Nature." *Urban Planning and Construction*, 2, no. 2, 1–24.

Sallis, J. 2012. *Logic of Imagination: The Expanse of the Elemental*. Bloomington: Indiana University Press.

Sartre, J. P. 2004. *The Imaginary: A Phenomenological Psychology of the Imagination*. Trans. J. Webber. New York: Routledge.

Scheler, M. 2008. *The Nature of Sympathy*. Trans. Peter Heath. London: Transaction.

Schmitz, O. J., Sylvén, M., Atwood, T. B. et al. 2023. "Trophic Rewilding Can Expand Natural Climate Solutions." *Nature Climate Change*, 13, 324–33.

Schneider-Mayerson, M. and B. R. Bellamy (Eds.). 2019. *An Ecotopian Lexicon*. Minneapolis: University of Minnesota Press.

Scholar, R. 2002. "La force de l'imagination de Montaigne: Camus, Malebranche, Pascal." *Littératures classiques*, 45, 127–38.

Schünemann, B., J. Keller, H. Rakoczy, et al. 2021. "Dogs Distinguish Human Intentional and Unintentional Action." *Scientific Report*, 11, 14967.

Sepper, D. L. 2015. *Understanding Imagination: The Reason of Images*. Dordrecht: Springer.

Shakespeare, W. 1979. *A Midsummer Night's Dream*. H. F. Brooks (ed.), *The Arden Shakespeare*, 2nd series. London: Methuen.
  2000. *The Tempest. A Case Study in Critical Controversy.* G. Graff and J. Phelan (eds.). Boston, NY: Bedford/St. Martin's.
Shettleworth, S. J. 1998. *Cognition, Evolution, and Behavior.* Oxford: Oxford University Press.
Smuts, B. 2002. "Gestural Communication in Olive Baboons and Domes-tic Dogs." In M. Bekoff, C. Allen, and G. Burghardt, (eds.), *The Cognitive Animal Empirical and Theoretical Perspectives on Animal Cognition.* Cambridge: The MIT Press, pp. 301–306.
  2021. "Encounters with. Animal Minds," *Journal of Consciousness Studies,* 8, 8-28.
Socha, K. 2013. "The 'Dreaded Comparisons' and Speciesism: Leveling the Hierarchy of Suffering." In K. Socha and S. Blum (eds.), *Confronting Animal Exploitation: Grassroots Essays on Liberation and Veganism.* Jefferson, NC: McFarland, 223-40.
Soper, K. 1995. *What is Nature?: Culture, Politics and the Non-Human.* Oxford and Cambridge: Blackwell.
Spiegel, M. 1996. *The Dreaded Comparison: Human and Animal Slavery.* New York: Mirror Books.
Spiller, E. 2009. "Shakespeare and the Making of Early Modern Science: Resituating Prospero's Art." *South Central Review,* 26, nos. 1 & 2 (Winter & Spring), 24–41.
Starhawk. 1982. *Dreaming the Dark: Magic, Sex, and Politics.* Boston, MA: Beacon Press.
  1988. *Truth or Dare: Encounters with Power, Authority, and Mystery.* New York: HarperCollins.
Stengers, I. 2002. "Une politique de l'hérésie entretien avec Isabelle Stengers." Interview by S. Grelet, P. Mangeot, and M. Potte-Bonneville. Vacarme, no. 19. April 2.
  2015. "Postface." Starhawk, *Rêver l'Obscur.* Paris: Cambourakis.
Sweet, E. L. and S. Ortiz Escalante. 2017. "Engaging territorio cuerpo-tierra through Body and Community Mapping: A Methodology for Making Communities Safer." *Gender, Place & Culture,* 24, no. 4, 594–606.
Thomashow, M. 2002. *Bringing the Biosphere Home: Learning to Perceive Global Environmental Change.* Cambridge, MA: MIT Press.
  2003. "What Is the Ecological Imagination?". *MitchellTomashow.com.* Accessed May 31, 2025. www.mitchelltomashow.com/blog/what-is-the-ecological-imagination.

Tinbergen, N. 1960. "The Natural Control of Insects in Pine Woods: Vol. I. Factors Influencing the Intensity of Predation by Songbirds." *Archives Neelandaises de Zoologie*, 13, (online).

Tribble, E. 2022. "'A Strange, Hollow, and Confused Noise': Prospero's 'Start' and Early Modern Magical Practices." *Shakespeare Quarterly*, 72, nos. 3–4 (Fall–Winter), 229-53.

Uexküll, J. von. 2010. *A Foray into the Worlds of Animals and Humans: With a Theory of Meaning*. Trans. J. D. O'Neil. Minneapolis: University of Minnesota Press.

Villanueva-Romero, D., L. Kerslake, and C. Flys-Junquera (eds.) 2021. *Imaginative Ecologies: Inspiring Change through the Humanities*. Leiden: Brill.

Volk, T. 2006. "Real Concerns, False Gods." *Nature*, 440, 869–70.

Westling, L. 2022. *Deep History, Climate Change, and the Evolution of Human Culture*. Elements in Environmental Humanities. Cambridge: Cambridge University Press.

Whiten, A. 2021. "The Burgeoning Reach of Animal Culture." *Science* 372, no. 6537, April 2.

Yusoff, K. 2019. *A Billion Black Anthropocenes or None*. Minneapolis: University Of Minnesota Press.

Zahavi, D. 2014. *Self and Other: Exploring Subjectivity, Empathy, and Shame*. Oxford: Oxford University Press.

Cambridge Elements ≡

Environmental Humanities

Louise Westling
University of Oregon

Louise Westling is an American scholar of literature and environmental humanities who was a founding member of the Association for the Study of Literature and Environment and its President in 1998. She has been active in the international movement for environmental cultural studies, teaching and writing on landscape imagery in literature, critical animal studies, biosemiotics, phenomenology, and deep history.

Serenella Iovino
University of North Carolina at Chapel Hill

Serenella Iovino is Professor of Italian Studies and Environmental Humanities at the University of North Carolina at Chapel Hill. She has written on a wide range of topics, including environmental ethics and ecocritical theory, bioregionalism and landscape studies, ecofeminism and posthumanism, comparative literature, eco-art, and the Anthropocene.

Timo Maran
University of Tartu

Timo Maran is an Estonian semiotician and poet. Maran is Professor of Ecosemiotics and Environmental Humanities and Head of the Department of Semiotics at the University of Tartu. His research interests are semiotic relations of nature and culture, Estonian nature writing, zoosemiotics and species conservation, and semiotics of biological mimicry.

About the Series

The environmental humanities is a new transdisciplinary complex of approaches to the embeddedness of human life and culture in all the dynamics that characterize the life of the planet. These approaches reexamine our species' history in light of the intensifying awareness of drastic climate change and ongoing mass extinction. To engage this reality, Cambridge Elements in Environmental Humanities builds on the idea of a more hybrid and participatory mode of research and debate, connecting critical and creative fields.

Cambridge Elements

Environmental Humanities

Elements in the Series

Climate Change Literacy
Julia Hoydis, Roman Bartosch and Jens Martin Gurr

Anthroposcreens: Mediating the Climate Unconscious
Julia Leyda

Aging Earth: Senescent Environmentalism for Dystopian Futures
Jacob Jewusiak

Blue Humanities: Storied Waterscapes in the Anthropocene
Serpil Oppermann

Nonhuman Subjects: An Ecology of Earth-Beings
Federico Luisetti

Indigenous Knowledge and Material Histories: The Example of Rubber
Jens Soentgen

The Open Veins of Modernity: Ecological Crisis and the Legacy of Byzantium and Pre-Columbian America
Eleni Kefala

Slime: An Elemental Imaginary
Simon C. Estok

Growing Hope: Narratives of Food Justice
Alexa Weik von Mossner

Descartes and the Non-human
Emma Gilby

Automobility and the Anthropocene: The Car as Post-Human
Gordon M. Sayre

The Earth Intoxicated on Imagination
Annabelle Dufourcq

A full series listing is available at: www.cambridge.org/EIEH

Printed by Integrated Books International,
United States of America